Correct
Grammar

Correct Grammar

by

Michael Cullup

Typeset in 11/12pt Times by Letterpart Limited.
Printed and bound in Great Britain by Cox & Wyman Limited, Reading, Berkshire.

Clarion: published from behind no. 80 Brighton Road, Tadworth, Surrey, England. For information about our company and the other books we publish, visit our website at
www.clarion-books.co.uk

Contents

1

Basics

The *grammar* of a particular language is the complete system which makes one language different from another. We know that German is different from French, for example. They sound different and, on the page, they look different. What makes them different is a matter of grammar. Their grammars are different.

It has been helpfully said that languages are 'rule governed'. That means that we can't just make them up anyhow and do what we like when we speak or write them. We know, much to our cost perhaps, that English has its own rather difficult and complicated spelling rules. If we want to check the way a word should be spelt, we can either look it up in a dictionary or use a computer spell-checker. And we can be confident that the spelling of the word will stay the same.

Syntax

There are other rules, too. If I write "cars blue" instead of "blue cars" you will immediately point out that the words are in the wrong order. The same would apply to "field in a under sky grass blue a cows". You can, after a struggle, decide what those words say, but in order to solve the problem you have to put the words into the right order. There are rules to do with the order of words in English (rules of *syntax*) just as there are rules concerning the order of letters in a word.

Although the order of letters in a word in English remains the same, the actual letters in the word may change. Take the word "house", for example. You know very well that if I write "six house" I am making a mistake. I am breaking one of the rules of English. In order to make what I write correct, I have to put an "s" on the word "house". That is one of the grammar rules of English. It's known as a rule of *inflection*.

But what about "Houses is nice to live in"? You know that I mean more than one house because I've put an "s" on the word "house", but you are not satisfied with the word "is". You are quite sure it should be "are". Another of the rules of English grammar is that we have to change "is" to "are" when we are talking about more than one thing. We call that *agreement* or *concord*.

Tenses
A sentence we would not expect to read in English would be: "I saw him tomorrow." And you could give two explanations. You could say that "tomorrow" should be changed to something like "yesterday" or "last week"; or that "saw" should be changed to "will see". These are yet more rules of English, and they concern the relationship between the *tense* of a *verb* and related *adverbs*.

By now, you may have noticed that when we talk about rules, we often mean making things agree with each other. We have to do the right thing, otherwise there will be chaos. But rather than referring to these matters as 'rules', it is sometimes easier to see them as 'customs'. And a lot of misunderstandings in language are solely caused because people, for various reasons, do not obey the customs in the language. It's the inability to do this, of course, which causes so much trouble when you try and understand someone who doesn't speak your language very well. It also explains the strange and mystified expressions on the faces of those people whose countries you visit when you go on holiday. For various reasons, you are not using the foreign language in the customary way.

But when we talk about the customary way of speaking a

language we're not just talking about grammar: we're also talking about *pronunciation*, for example. When you listen to speakers of English on television, you can usually understand the people who speak like your English teachers, but others are very difficult to understand.

Accent and Dialect

There are two possibilities here. The first concerns *accent* and the second concerns *dialect*. You might be having problems understanding someone because the accent is very strange to you; and you might be having further problems for reasons of dialect. 'Dialect' involves more than just pronunciation. It involves grammar as well. The person speaking to you may seem to be using a different grammar. In addition, the person may be using words you aren't familiar with: the *vocabulary* or *lexis* may be different. So, if the dialect is very strong – and strange to you – you will certainly have a serious problem. This doesn't mean that a foreign sounding dialect of English is, in fact, a foreign *language*. It isn't. A dialect is a dialect of a particular language. It's related to a parent language. Some of the rules are different, but they aren't different enough for the dialect to be considered a completely different language. When the difference is purely one of accent – saying "but" to rhyme with "foot" in English, for example – things aren't too difficult. But when the order of words, or the actual words used are also different, then we are dealing with a dialect rather than just an accent.

Sometimes, writers try to show how other accents sound by using special spellings. Occasionally it works with English, but usually it doesn't. If you look at a sentence in Italian, in a phrase-book, you'll find that you can say the words quite easily from the spelling. But imagine you're an Italian trying to pronounce the spelling "night"! And what about "though", "through", "trough", "enough"?

We call the study of sounds in a language *phonetics*, and a special alphabet, called the *phonetic alphabet*, has been devised. If you've ever seen it – and you can find it used in good dictionaries – you'll see that it looks rather different from the ordinary English alphabet. It's not necessary to learn this alphabet, though it can be learned quite easily. The point is that it allows people to write down exactly how a word is said, so that other people who know the phonetic alphabet can say the word.

Pronunciation

Pronunciation isn't just sounds, however. In some languages, people seem to sing and we tend to call such languages 'musical'. But this singing occurs in English too. And we call this music *intonation*. We can recognise it when an English person asks a question. Asking questions has a different music from answering them. The intonation is different.

When we look at spellings, by the way, we divide the letters into two kinds: *consonants*, which includes all of the letters in the alphabet except the *vowels*. In English, there are only five vowels: a, e, i, o, u. People trying to learn English find that the vowels and some of the consonants sound strange and often seem in the wrong part of the word.

Listen, also, to the way you pronounce the word "rebel" when you say these two sentences: "The rebel surrendered his gun" and "Adolescents always seem to rebel against their parents". In the first sentence, the first part of the word seems strong or loud; in the second sentence, it's the last part that sounds strong. Technically, we say that in the first "rebel" the *stress* is on the first part, and in the second the stress is on the last part. Notice, also, that both words sound as if they have two parts, whereas the word "adolescent" has four. We call each part a *syllable*. So, we can say that in our first sentence, "rebel" has the stress on the first syllable, and in our second sentence "rebel" has the stress on the second, or last, syllable.

The important thing is to understand what technical terms mean. If you can explain them clearly and simply to someone else, then you really understand them. If you can't, have a another think about them. Be convinced that grammar can be quite straightforward and comprehensible even if, at first, it all looks rather forbidding.

But we do have to be sensitive about this matter of customs. All of us know that different societies have different customs. All of us know that travelling abroad means, to some extent, learning to adapt to customs which are unfamiliar. That, after all, is why we speak of 'foreign' countries. They are unfamiliar, and their customs are unfamiliar.

It's just the same with languages. Languages other than our own are 'foreign' languages. We can't behave in these languages as if they were our own. They have, above all, different grammars. Yet we can't even begin to talk about these matters until we've learned the necessary vocabulary for the bits and pieces and the necessary technical terms for the rules.

Next time, we'll look into this business in more detail. But first, overleaf are the important terms you have been introduced to so far:

New Grammatical Terms (1)

accent the sounds different speakers make when they speak the same language

adverb a word which is closely related to a verb

agreement or concord the special grammatical spellings which show how certain words belong with other words

consonants vocal sounds which are interrupted in some way by the lips, tongue and teeth

dialect a branch of the same language which has differences of pronunciation and grammar

grammar the complete system of rules which makes one language different from another

inflection the special grammatical ending on a word

intonation the musical rise and fall of sounds in a language

language a means of communication which has its own distinctive grammar

phonetic alphabet an alphabet which represents the sounds in a language

phonetics the study of language sounds

pronunciation the sounds we make when we speak a language

stress where one part of a word or group of words is made to sound stronger than others

syllables the parts into which a word is divided when spoken

syntax the order of words

tense changes to a verb to show how it relates to time

verb a word which activates other words by causing things to happen in time

vocabulary or lexis the words in a language

vowels uninterrupted vocal sounds

Revision One

Here are some descriptions. See if you can tell what the descriptions refer to:

1. Without one of these, a sentence would say very little. For example, no-one would do anything, or feel anything, or see anything.
2. Connected with a particular language, but having a non-standard pronunciation and some differences in grammar and vocabulary.
3. Making a word, for example, especially strong.
4. The ending on a word which sometimes changes.
5. The rules of a particular language.
6. The sounds of a language.
7. Another word for vocabulary.
8. Sounds which are released without interruption from, for example, the tongue or teeth.
9. The way the sounds in a language go up and down.
10. Something which is closely connected with a verb.
11. The means through which human beings communicate.
12. Separate parts of words.
13. The order of words.
14. The way we show in a language that certain words have to agree grammatically with other words.
15. The aspect of verbs which relates to time.
16. When we speak, these sounds are affected by our tongue, teeth, and lips.
17. A special alphabet which contains a symbol for each different sound in a language or languages.
18. The way we speak a particular language.
19. How some speakers pronounce a particular language.

Key (Revision 1)

1. Verb.
2. Dialect.
3. Stress.
4. Inflection.
5. Grammar.
6. Phonetics.
7. Lexis.
8. Vowels.
9. Intonation.
10. Adverb.
11. Language.
12. Syllables.
13. Syntax.
14. Agreement or concord.
15. Tense.
16. Consonants.
17. Phonetic alphabet.
18. Pronunciation.
19. Accent.

2

Nuts and Bolts

When you talk about a language it's very useful to be able to use the names of the various bits and pieces. Then, we do at least know what we're talking about.

In the past, they used to use the term *parts of speech* to mean all these various bits of speech. It's not a good term really because it's hard to imagine these bits and pieces as parts of what someone says. It's far easier to think about them by looking at what someone writes. That doesn't mean to say that writing is more important than speaking. Far from it. Most people want to learn a foreign language in order to be able to speak it rather than write it. Unfortunately, however, the job is made a lot easier if we can read the language too, as well as reading descriptions of how it works.

If we are to be able to read about the language we are trying to learn, then we need to know what the little bits and pieces are called. In order to learn the names of these bits and pieces, let's consider the words on this page. Each one belongs to a particular type. We've already met adverbs and verbs, to name only two types, although only very briefly and superficially. And both of these have been described by the work that they do. But let's, for the moment, forget about adverbs and verbs and concentrate on *nouns*.

Nouns
Nouns are, if you like, the basic things we see around us. The chair we're sitting on, the picture we can see on the

wall, the door, the settee, the table, the radiator, the carpet. You could go on and on making a list of all these things, and they would all be nouns. But, if you think about it, there are other things we come across which we can't see and touch. We can feel them but we can't see them, even if we have normal vision. Take love, for example, or fear, or anger. These are all nouns, but we can't see the three of them. We can see an expression (also a noun) on someone's face, but not fear itself.

It's very important to spend quite a lot of time thinking about nouns, because they behave in a special way in different languages. Nouns in different languages are still called nouns, and that goes for grammatical terms in general. But the behaviour of different types of words in different languages is different. There are different rules about where you put them, how you change them, and so on.

Gender
In some languages, like French, the chairs and tables and pictures and other things are regarded as either male or female. If a noun in a foreign language is male, we call it a *masculine* noun; if it's female, we call it *feminine*; if it's neither, we call it *neuter*. We need to know which one it is in certain languages because in those languages feminine nouns behave in a different way from masculine nouns, for example.

Concrete or abstract
Anyway, here we are then in a world of nouns: things we can see and touch, and things we can't see and touch. We call the things we *can* see and touch *concrete* nouns, and we call the things we *can't* see and touch *abstract* nouns.

Babies begin to talk by naming the things around them. We know that they use nouns to do this. Over a few weeks babies can add quite a lot of concrete nouns to their vocabulary. Sooner or later, however, even small toddlers need to use abstract nouns. And we adults can't do without them. We talk about politics, sport, religion, holidays, pensions and work – all things we can't actually see and touch. And to talk about these things we mix our nouns with other types of words which obviously aren't 'things'. Words like "the" and "of" and "fed up".

Adjectives

Perhaps the most important types of words after nouns are what we call *adjectives*. They allow us to describe nouns. So we can use colours, for example. And all colours are adjectives. We talk about a "red" sofa, a "green" door, a "black" car. Notice that, in English, we can put the adjective immediately in front of the noun. In many languages they can't do this. There is a different rule about using adjectives in those languages. The rule in English is "you can put the adjective immediately in front of the noun" but in some languages the rule is "you can't put the adjective immediately in front of the noun."

A lot of adjectives are rather like concrete nouns. We can actually see if something is "red", or "big", or "long", or "wide". And we can easily feel if something is "heavy" or "light". We can taste if something is "sweet" or "sour". We can feel if something is "rough" or "smooth". In fact, a lot of adjectives have to do with our senses.

But not all. A "happy" wedding, a "sad" funeral, or an "exciting" adventure are rather different. Adjectives like "happy", "sad", and "exciting" can't be tested in the same way as the adjectives in the previous paragraph. People don't normally disagree about "red" and "green" or "rough" and "smooth", but they often do about "happy" and "sad". "I thought it was a boring film," says one. "Did you?" says another. "I thought it was very exciting." And when we get to adjectives like "complicated", "simple", "sophisticated", "mathematical", and so on, life is once more getting rather abstract. But all these adjectives can still go in front of their nouns.

However, we don't always put them there. Sometimes we say that "it is a red carpet"; sometimes we say that "the carpet is red". The adjective "red" is still describing the carpet, though. And that is what adjectives do: they describe things. If you think about it, we wouldn't get far if all we could do was name the things around us. We need, so often, to describe what they are like. Imagine someone coming home and saying "There's a carpet in the shop". It's not enough, is it? Which shop? What colour? What size? We need adjectives to add description to the carpet, otherwise we have no idea about what the carpet is like. And the same goes for all the things around us, all the feelings we have, all the things that happen in our lives. We need adjectives to bring all these things to life. Very often, the good storyteller is the person who is skilled in the use of adjectives.

Notice, by the way, that although adjectives are easy to recognise when they come in front of nouns, we aren't calling them adjectives simply because they are often found in that position. We call them adjectives because of what they do. They describe. It's easy to get caught out in grammar by not thinking enough about what a type of word actually does. We call that its *function*. And the function of adjectives is to describe. In the sentence "I feel sick", the adjective is "sick". It's as simple as that. Don't get worried because the adjective is at the end, or because you can't find a noun anywhere.

Sentences
But what about the groups of words where we find nouns and adjectives? Is there a name for different groups of words? Yes, there is. For the moment, however, it's best to stick with the group we are all familiar with and that we know best: the *sentence*. It's easy to recognise because it usually has a full-stop or question mark after it. We can find all our word types in particular sentences, although not every sentence, of course, contains every type of word. We can certainly expect to find nouns in most written sentences, since it's hard to talk about things without mentioning the things we want to talk about!

It would also be rather odd if all we did was go around

uttering only nouns and adjectives. We would certainly sound like small toddlers if that was all we did. Imagine a world in which adults could only say "Red chair!" "Nice chips!" "Good book!" We need to do rather more than that to be fully human. And in order to do more than that we need *verbs*.

Verbs

Verbs make things happen! They bring the world we describe to life. Birds sing in the trees, the sun shines, we open the window and the fresh air flows in. We're so happy, we dance and sing and clap our hands.

The words "sing", "shines", "open", "flows", "dance", and "clap" are all verbs. Verbs, I hasten to add, are rather complicated. And that's putting it mildly. We *shall* look more closely at verbs, but all in good time. For the moment, let's concentrate on learning to identify what they are.

In some text-books, verbs are still described as "doing words". This is helpful up to a point, but it can lead to a lot of confusion when we begin to come across verbs which certainly don't seem to do much. However, like all things in grammar, descriptions and definitions are commonly incomplete. We have to get used to this. An expert in linguistics, reading this book, would be the first to emphasise that I had only told half the story. But I believe that it doesn't do to burden ourselves with the philosophical complexities of linguistics. We want to learn the basics of grammar, either for practical reasons or for our own personal amusement. If some of us want to go deeper into the subject, all well and good, but most of us will be content with a good basic knowledge.

So, what about these verbs then? If they aren't just "doing words" then what are they? One useful way of describing them would be to say, as I've already suggested, that they bring nouns and adjectives to life. They help to complete the story which nouns and adjectives begin. Without verbs nothing happens, nothing moves; stories can't be told.

Can we do without verbs?

Just try to tell a story without verbs. It might go something like this: "One day, I .... on a bench when I .... something strange .... A tiny bird .... down out of a tree and .... a huge Alsatian dog. The dog .... fiercely and .... at the bird, but the little bird .... away and .... in the least."

Isn't it frustrating? So much is missing. But the bits that are missing can all be filled in with verbs. When we've done that, we have a story. But not until. Here's a full story, with all the verbs put in.

"One day, I was sitting on a bench when I saw something strange happen. A tiny bird flew down out of a tree and pecked a huge Alsatian dog. The dog growled fiercely and rushed at the bird, but the little bird flew away and didn't seem to mind in the least."

If we make a list of the verbs, we find it rather difficult to match them together. They seem so different, somehow. Here's the list: "was sitting", "saw", "happen", "flew", "pecked", "growled", "rushed", "flew", "didn't seem", "to mind". What a mixture! Although most of them consist of one word, three of them consist of two words. Some end in "-ed" but others end in almost anything.

Past, present and future

We know more about this list of verbs than we think. We're not going to tackle the whole business of verbs yet: it's too complicated. But we can easily pick out all the verbs which are about the past. Try it, and see what happens.

All of us picked out "was sitting", "saw", "flew", "pecked", "growled", "rushed", "didn't". There was nothing difficult about that, was there? We say, in grammar, that all these verbs are in the *past*.

If we care to think about it just a little longer, we might go on to think that, if some verbs are in the past, then some must be in the *present* and some in the *future*. Life isn't all about the past, after all. We are doing things now and we shall do other things tomorrow.

Nevertheless, however obvious this is, we may still be confused about which words are verbs and which aren't. But are we, perhaps, a little less confident than we deserve to be? Just take the words in the previous paragraph. How many verbs do you think there are? Try counting them.

If you counted more than ten, you were certainly on the right lines. Not all verbs are easy to identify, but there's something about verbs which makes identifying them easier as you get more practice. And, of course, when we've looked at verbs in rather more detail, we shall, I hope, find them relatively easy to pick out and describe.

Now let's leave verbs for the time being and look at some of the other words we find in a lot of sentences. But, before we do so, overleaf are the new terms you have been introduced to in this chapter:

New Grammatical Terms (2)

abstract used of nouns which are not physical

adjectives words which describe things

concrete used of nouns which stand for physical things

feminine words regarded as female

function the purpose of a part of speech

future anything after now

masculine words regarded as male

neuter words regarded as neither

nouns words which stand for things

parts of speech the terms by which we define words according to their grammatical function

past anything before now

present now

sentence a group of words which, in writing, begins with a capital letter and ends with a full-stop

Revision Two

See if you can fill in the gaps in this description:

When we look at a language, and especially its grammar, we tend to concentrate on groups of words which, in writing, begin with a capital letter and end with a full-stop. We call these groups of words (a) .... These groups of words contain verbs, which have changes of tense to show whether, in time, they refer to the (b) .... (c) ...... or (d) .... But verbs are not the only (e) .... in sentences. We can also find describing words, called (f) .... and, most importantly, words which refer principally to things and which we call (g) .... These words which refer to things can, in some languages, be spelled differently according to whether they refer to things which are regarded as male, female, or neither. Things which are female are called (h) .... Things which are male are called (i) .... And things which are neither are called (j) .... When looking at words which refer to things, we must also consider whether we are talking about actual things in the physical world or non-material qualities and things of that nature. Things which occur in the physical world are called (k) .... and things which don't are called (l) ...... But whatever these different terms for different elements in the grammar, we must concentrate on what they do – their (m) .... – more than anything else.

Key (Revision 2)

(a) sentences
(b) past*
(c) present*
(d) future*
    (* these last three can be in any order)
(e) parts of speech
(f) adjectives
(g) nouns
(h) feminine
(i) masculine
(j) neuter
(k) concrete
(l) abstract
(m) function

3

Sorting Things Out

Already the technical terms are beginning to build up. As they do, try and keep a kind of picture in mind. It's a picture of language itself, in all its manifestations, and it's so complex and diverse that it demands sorting out in some way. Until we've at least begun to do that, how can we possibly know what sort of animal we are trying to understand?

"Table" as an example
Let's begin with a single word. "Table", for instance. In isolation, all we might be expected to know from the word is that it refers to a piece of furniture. But, in some languages, we would know it was female because of its spelling: it would have a feminine ending, for example. In English this is not the case.

"Her" and "she"
It might occur to us that, in English, there are two different words which refer to a female: the word "she" and the word "her". How are these two words different?

If I made the sentence "Her is a woman", you would immediately tell me the word should be "she". On the other hand, if I made the sentence "That's she", you would immediately tell me the word should be "her". But why?

In the sentence "She is the woman who spoke to her" we are referring to two women. We can't say "She is the woman who spoke to she" or "Her is the woman who spoke to her". If we do, there is no way of distinguishing one of the women from the other. One of the women is more important than the other, and we refer to that woman as "she". This is, if you like, the woman we are most interested in. She is the subject of our conversation, and it so happens that we call the most important person in our sentence the *subject*. And in this particular sentence, the woman to whom our subject speaks is called the *object*.

In this case, we are fortunate enough to have two spellings for the woman: one for the woman as subject and one for the woman as object. But, generally, in English we have no special spellings for these *grammatical categories*. In a sentence like "The dog bit the dog", there is no difference in spelling between the subject and the object. We could say, technically, that there is no inflection here. Or we could say that, in English, nouns are not normally inflected for *gender*, meaning that they don't have special spellings to show whether they are masculine or feminine.

Pronouns

Pronouns, then, are inflected. But what are pronouns? Well, "she" and "her" are examples of pronouns. And if you look at the word "pronoun" itself, you will see that it begins with the *prefix* "pro-" which means "on behalf of" or "instead". Pronouns are used instead of nouns when, for example, repeating the noun again and again would become irritating and monotonous. "John drove home and John parked John's car in John's drive and then went into John's house where John's wife was waiting for John" is a tedious way of saying that "John drove home and he parked his car in his drive and then went into his house where his wife was waiting for him." We would find it laborious to struggle on without both kinds of pronouns: *personal*, to do with people, and *impersonal*, to do with things. We don't normally call a person "it".

Inflection

Nouns are inflected to show whether there is one of them or more than one. That is, they are inflected to show *number*: whether they are *singular* or *plural*. They are also inflected to show possession. The name ''John'', for example, is a noun. If we want to talk about something belonging to John we can say ''John's''.

Pronouns, however, are rich in inflection. ''I'', ''me'', ''mine''; ''she'', ''her'', ''hers''; ''it'', ''its''; ''they'', ''them'', ''their'' and so on. You can probably think of lots of them. ''She has a sister, but her sister doesn't speak to her.'' Here we have an example of the personal pronoun as subject, as object, and as a *possessive*.

It's no use pretending that we don't need these distinctions. We do. If they weren't there, things would be all of a jumble. The very fact that words are spelt differently from each other means that they are, in fact, different words. If this were not the case, there would be problems. Some of the differences are very small but, as with spellings which show grammatical differences, we have to be aware of them because there are differences of meaning, or *semantic* differences. A ''chair'' is obviously different from a ''settee''. And the words, too, are very different: they each contain completely different letters of the alphabet. We can, perhaps, begin to realise the important difference between words such as ''there'' and ''their'', ''reefer'' and ''refer'', ''pet'' and ''pit'', especially where the difference in spelling is so very small.

Phonemes

We have to distinguish differences in sounds, too. The words ''pet'' and ''pit'' contain different vowel sounds, and it is these vowel sounds, and these alone, which show us that these words are different. In every language, there is a fixed number of different sounds which are used to distinguish words, and these sounds are called *phonemes*. The two vowel sounds in ''pet'' and ''pit'' are two of the phonemes in the English language. And there are consonants, too, which are phonemes of English. The difference between "pet" and "let" is shown by two other English phonemes: the consonants which begin the two words. If these phonemes did not exist in English, then we would not be able to distinguish these very different words. And if we don't pronounce these words properly, then we cannot effectively communicate what we want to communicate. Our listeners must be able to hear the difference between these words when we say them.

Pronunciation

In English, we have a generally accepted *standard pronunciation* of the language. It used to be regarded as the kind of pronunciation used by BBC announcers. Sometimes, quite erroneously, such a pronunciation was referred to as "Oxford English". But that was to miss the point: the idea of a standard pronunciation was to have a form of English pronunciation which was understood by everybody who knew the language. If agreement could be reached on what this form was, then it could be taught in schools and adopted as a norm. Unfortunately, the issue has become clouded with political emotions but, even so, most of us would accept that the idea of a standard pronunciation is both practical and helpful.

We have, of course, a standard spelling for words, in spite of small differences between British spelling and the spelling used in the United States. And though these differences are interesting, they are hardly worth making much of. Pronunciation differences, on the other hand, are much more important and can cause considerable problems. Because of the printed word, spelling is highly consistent throughout the world and simply has to be learned and followed.

Back to syntax again!

But to return to our sentence. We have already seen the usefulness of our inflected pronouns. However, because English is not, as are so many languages, a highly inflected language, the order of words, or syntax, is extremely

28

important. We do need to know what is the subject of our sentence and what is its object. We do need to know that when we write ''The dog bit the dog'' we are talking about two different dogs: the dog which did the biting (the subject) and the dog which was bitten (the object). And, since the noun ''dog'' is not inflected, the rule in English is that the dog which comes first is regarded as the subject and the dog which comes after the verb is regarded as the object.

There are other syntactical rules, too. In English syntax, the adjective comes before the noun. We say ''blue sky'' and not ''sky blue''. And, normally but not always, the adverb comes after the verb: ''walked quickly'' and not ''quickly walked''. By keeping to these rules, or customs, we all know more or less where we are. And, before we go on to explore the sentence in more detail, we need to accept that there are rules and that we do need to follow them.

To finish, overleaf are the new terms we have come across in this chapter:

New Grammatical Terms (3)

gender whether a word is regarded as masculine, feminine, or neuter

grammatical category how we define a word or group of words in our grammar of the language

impersonal concerning things

number whether singular or plural

object who or what is affected by the subject

personal concerning people

phoneme a particular sound in a language

plural more than one

possessive belonging to

prefix something added to the beginning of a word

pronoun a word used instead of a noun

semantic to do with meaning

singular only one

standard pronunciation the kind of pronunciation which is regarded as normal or generally acceptable

subject who or what a sentence is about

Revision Three

Try and answer these questions. You can write the answers down or, if you like, think of the answer then consult the key on page 33.

1. What is the word we prefer to use when we are talking about 'meaning'?

2. A noun is sometimes described as the name of a place, person, or thing. What kind of word do we use when we want to replace a noun, perhaps because we want to avoid tedious repetition?

3. In 2, the part of speech that we use can be of two types, depending on whether we are referring to things or to people. What are the two types?

4. Nouns can refer to either one thing or more than one thing. In other words they can be what?

5. They can also be inflected to show whether we are talking about what belongs to them. What is the technical word for this kind of situation?

6. There are some sounds which are crucial in determining the difference between two words in a language. What do we call these sounds?

7. When we add something to the beginning of a word, what do we call this new part?

8. Every sentence must have something which comes before the verb and without which we have nothing really to talk about. In some languages the noun in this part has a special inflection. What is this part of a sentence called?

9. Nouns in some languages can also be inflected to show that they represent something which is affected rather than something which starts an action. What do we call this type of noun?

10. In order to study a language, we can divide the words in a sentence into their various parts of speech. But we can study the language in far greater depth by using the full range of descriptive terms. What do we call these terms, or divisions?

11. In some languages a word can be masculine, feminine, or neuter. When we talk about this kind of difference what are we talking about?

12. When we are talking about whether a noun refers to one or more than one thing, we are talking about what?
13. What do we call a way of speaking which is generally acceptable among speakers of that language?

Key (Revision 3)

1. Semantic(s).
2. Pronoun.
3. Impersonal and personal.
4. Singular or plural.
5. Possession (possessive).
6. Phonemes.
7. A prefix.
8. The subject.
9. The object.
10. Grammatical categories.
11. Gender.
12. Number.
13. Standard pronunciation.

4

Parts of the Sentence

Like almost everything one cares to think of, sentences can be divided into their separate parts. The experts tend to argue about what these separate parts of a sentence are, and how small each part should be. But there is enough agreement about it all to keep us happy. It's worth knowing, however, that there are different grammars with different ideas about this kind of thing. So don't get the idea that the truth has forever been discovered and all differences laid to rest. Try and keep a reasonably open mind, and don't be distressed if you find some contradictions. But, before we can break up our sentences, we have first to decide what a sentence is.

So, what is a sentence?
Sentences have been variously described, and all of us have come across definitions of some kind or other. They vary from the utterly confusing (''A sentence is a complete thought in words'') to the uselessly obvious (''A sentence begins with a capital letter and ends with a full-stop'').

If you care to think about it for a moment, you might decide that all this is a bit philosophical really. After all, when we speak, we just speak. We don't think about sentences at all. In fact, it's hard to think of sentences being in there somewhere. What we hear is a stream of words, with pauses for breath or thought. What we say is what comes into our heads as we feel, or think, or whatever it is. All this language comes out, with not a thought about forming it all into sentences.

But writing is different

Yet it isn't quite the same with writing. As we write, we have to separate the words, for a start. We can't simply join all the letters together to make one long word. It's interesting to notice that if you listen to a foreign language you don't understand, a lot of it does seem to consist of words all joined up together. And, in fact, when we ourselves speak our own language, we do run the words into each other.

Spoken words, as we know, are made up of vowels and consonants and divided up into syllables. When we talk about written words, we still use the same terms but prefer to make it clear that we are talking about the letters of the alphabet. There are certain combinations of vowels which we call *diphthongs* and it can be quite confusing if we use this term to refer to the written letters. Strictly speaking, diphthongs are sound combinations. In the word "late", two vowel sounds come together to make one diphthong, but the spelling only shows the letter "a". In some words, two letters are used together to make one vowel sound, as in the word "thief". When we use the phonetic alphabet to represent the vowel sound in the word "thief", there is no problem, but writing is rather different.

The written sentence

It's important to get these matters clear, before we begin to talk about the parts of the written sentence in more detail. We are not talking about spoken language: we are talking about the written language only. The spoken language has received a great deal of study from specialists in linguistics, and rightly so. But for the time being at least, we are concentrating on the written sentence.

Words, then, are composed of letters of the alphabet. Above the level of letters, linguistics uses the term *morpheme* to describe the smallest unit of meaning within a word. Unfortunately, this is complex and difficult and, to us at least, not particularly useful. Basically, the term is used to talk about things like the endings of words to show plurals, which we have called 'inflections', and the change, for example, from ''man'' to the plural ''men''.

We have to accept that, to talk about language and grammar in depth, specialists have to invent new terms. This happens in all the sciences. But not all these terms are of use to us. The term 'morpheme' is no use at all, but the term 'inflection' is invaluable. The term 'syllable' is very useful, but we must make sure not to mix the written and the spoken language.

Each word listed in a dictionary is called an *entry*. This is because words with the same spelling are sometimes listed more than once. Two words spelt the same with different meanings, called *homonyms*, normally have separate entries but, if the meanings are related, each different meaning is numbered and kept with the main entry.

If the long words in our dictionary have been split up into parts, we must remember that this kind of thing is relevant only to the spoken language. Normally this is made quite clear by using the phonetic alphabet. There may, however, be other information about the grammar of the word which is particularly useful for the written language. We may be told what part of speech the word is and how to form other parts of speech from it, or make it plural. In fact, a good dictionary contains a lot of very useful grammatical information. But we'll come to that later.

For the time being, we'll take our sentences as being composed of different words, some *monosyllabic* (one syllable) and some *polysyllabic* (more than one syllable). These words are strung out in a line across the page. Some of the words begin with capitals but most don't. There seems to be a habit of using full-stops from time to time, as well.

When the writer of these sentences uses a full-stop, the intention is to show that what the writer considers as a sentence is finished. The same writer will probably put a capital letter at the beginning of each sentence. If the writer doesn't, then we won't be sure of where the writer wants us to recognise the beginning of the sentence.

But – and this is a very large 'but' – the decision to mark the beginning and ending of the sentences is the writer's responsibility. And if we know the conventions, and the writer does as well, then we shall be on fairly safe ground.

There will still be difficulties, however. When we see a single word with a full-stop after it, surely it can't be a complete sentence? And some sentences have a hundred words or more in them!

This is probably where those of us who were taught grammar at school first became confused. The teacher kept bringing in things which weren't there in front of us. The single word was explained as meaning rather more than just a single word: as meaning, in fact, a complete sentence. So, "Silence." meant "There was silence" or "I couldn't hear anything". And, of course, our teacher was right. The words in front of us are an attempt at meaning, and we have to learn to interpret them.

Now, let's accept that this sentence business is complicated, but let's also accept that we need to start somewhere. We need, in fact, to take some things for granted.

The first thing we'll take for granted is that our writer knows all about where to put capital letters and full-stops – which is something we'll be learning about later. We also need to assume that the writer knows how to form sentences according to the grammatical rules of the language. Having accepted those two basic points, let's begin to break the sentence down a bit.

Breaking down the sentence
At the very heart of the sentence is the verb. In English, this tends to come at the end of a group of words or in the middle. It doesn't normally come at the beginning. What comes at the beginning is the subject of the verb, which is always a noun, pronoun, or equivalent group. So, basically, a group of words which, together, make a simple sentence in English will contain a subject and a verb. Simple sentences are sentences like: "He laughed."; "The woman disappeared."; "The dog barked.".

Simple sentences can contain more than that, however.

They can contain words which come after the verb. These words are commonly *objects*: "The dog bit the man". And the objects are, again, nouns or pronouns. But we don't always call this third part of a simple sentence 'the object'. This is because some verbs can't have objects. A typical example is the verb "to be". We can "hit" or "bite" something, but we can't "is" it. So, after some verbs, we talk about *complements* rather than objects.

If we look at the sentence "The dog bit the man", we notice two extra words: one before the word "dog" and one before the word "man". We call these *articles*.

Left as it is, our sentence is rather matter-of-fact. To make it more interesting, we can put adjectives in front of the nouns to describe both the dog and the man. We could also put an adverb after the object "man" to describe how the dog bit the man: "badly", for instance. And we could build our sentence up even further.

Subject and predicate
For the time being, however, we want to keep the basic shape in mind: subject, verb, object; or subject, verb, complement. We can divide the sentence up even more simply into subject and *predicate*. Here, the predicate is all the words that come after the subject.

When you look at sentences – the ones on this page, for instance – each sentence looks very complicated. But try and see each sentence as having at least a subject and a verb. Without these two, it couldn't commonly be a sentence. Let's look at one of the sentences in more detail. Let's look at the sentence: "We can divide the sentence up even more simply into subject and predicate".

Here, the subject is quite simply "we". The verb is "can divide up" and the object is "the sentence". There are complications: we had to join the word "up" with "can divide" to make the full verb and we ignored all the words that came after the object. We shall be learning more about verbs in Chapters 7 and 8 so, for the time being, don't worry too much about that three-part verb. Simply accept the fact that there is a clear subject, verb, and object here.

Dividing it up a bit further

But what about the bit that comes after the object? What do we call that? Well, we could regard everything after the subject as the predicate but, since we have picked out the object of the sentence, we have begun to break the predicate up. So, let's look further at the words: "even more simply into subject and predicate".

First of all, we don't really want to venture into 'parts of speech' territory. The reason for this is that we are not breaking the sentence down that finely. We are, for the moment, trying to group words rather than treat them singly. However, it is important to see that "even more simply" describes how the sentence can be "divided up". Because the words tell us 'how' something is done, they relate directly to the verb. We therefore regard these words as *adverbial*. Because they are a 'group' of words, we refer to the group as a *phrase*.

If we now take this *adverbial phrase* out, we are left with "into subject and predicate". This group of words begins with the preposition "into" and we therefore refer to it as a *prepositional phrase*. Words like "in", "on", "at", "to", "from", and so on, are called *prepositions*, and we shall learn more about them in later chapters.

We have now broken down our sentence into its constituent parts: a subject and a predicate which can be further broken down into a verb, an object, an adverbial phrase and a prepositional phrase.

Admittedly, this is a bit difficult, if only because we don't yet know much about the various parts of speech. But as we go on, everything will hopefully tend to clarify as the picture gets filled in. The important thing to understand in this chapter is the way a sentence can be broken down into parts.

Most sentences contain more than one verb. Sometimes a part of a sentence can look rather like a sentence itself. In fact, parts of sentences can often stand alone as separate sentences. In the sentence "The little boy played with the dog and the little girl helped her father", we could have two sentences: "The little boy played with the dog" would be one, and "The little girl helped her father" would be the other. In the longer sentence, we have two sentences joined to make one with the *conjunction*, or joining word, "and".

Clauses

When these sentences occur within sentences, we can't call them 'sentences' any more. Instead, we call them *clauses*. Clauses always have to contain verbs, otherwise they become phrases. And because the clauses we are speaking about can stand independently, they are always called *main clauses* and they occur in *complex sentences*. In cases where there are two clauses which we could call 'main clauses', we regard them as equal and call them *co-ordinate clauses*. Our sentences are separated by a conjunction, so we call that kind of sentence a *compound sentence*.

All this is rather a lot to take in, I know, but the next two chapters should gradually help to make it all clearer. In the mean time, here are the terms we have come across in this chapter:

New Grammatical Terms (4)

adverbial to do with adverbs, often expressing how something is done

adverbial phrase (see above)

articles words which come just before nouns, like "the", "a", and "an"

clause a group of words containing a verb

complement what comes after, and goes with, a verb which doesn't have objects

complex sentence a sentence having more than one clause

compound sentence a sentence which contains two equal clauses

conjunction a word like "and", joining single words or groups of words

co-ordinate clauses two main clauses separated by a conjunction

diphthong two vowel sounds coming together to make one

entry a word separately entered in a dictionary

homonyms two words spelt the same but with different meanings

main clause a clause which could stand on its own as a sentence

monosyllabic having only one syllable

morpheme the smallest unit of meaning within a word

phrase a group of words without a verb

polysyllabic having more than one syllable

predicate everything that comes after the subject

prepositional phrase a phrase beginning with a preposition

prepositions words like "on", "in", "of"

Revision Four

See if you can answer these questions:

1. What would you call two vowels combined?
2. What is the difference between a phrase and a clause?
3. What is the difference between the object and the predicate in a sentence?
4. Do all verbs have objects?
5. What do we call words like "in" and "to"?
6. What are homonyms?
7. What do you call phrases which begin with an adverb?
8. How can you tell a prepositional phrase?
9. What is the difference between a simple, a complex, and a compound sentence?
10. What are co-ordinate clauses joined by?
11. What is a main clause?
12. What is a word listed separately in a dictionary called?

Key (Revision 4)

1. A diphthong.
2. A clause has a verb but a phrase doesn't.*
3. The predicate is everything that comes after the subject, but the object comes after the verb.
4. No. Some, like the verb "to be", have complements. And some, like "disappear", have neither.
5. Prepositions.
6. They are words which are spelled the same but which have different meanings.
7. Adverbial phrases.
8. It begins with a preposition.
9. A simple sentence consists of only one clause. A complex sentence has more than one clause. A compound sentence consists of two equal clauses.
10. They are joined by a conjunction.
11. A clause in a sentence which could stand on its own as a sentence.
12. An entry.

* This is not strictly true, but will do for the time being. We shall learn more about this in Chapters 7 and 8.

5

Building the Sentence

We now need to look more closely into how we actually build our sentences up. Much of what can be said about this is directly related to what we learned in the previous chapter.

There is always a subject
What we learned was that the sentence always has a subject, and this is the case even if the subject is not directly mentioned. In such cases, we say that the subject is 'understood'. When a character in a story, for instance, shouts "Silence!", we should know by the context who is speaking, or shouting, to whom. In this particular case, we have to rebuild our sentence from this information. But we still call this a sentence even though we have to build the sentence for ourselves.

This isn't, of course, something we have to worry about when we are writing our own sentences. Normally, we know who or what we are writing about, and then carry on from there. Our subject need not be a single noun: it can be a noun phrase or a noun clause. If I write a sentence like "The subject of this essay is 'Growing Vegetables' ", then everything before the verb "is" can be regarded as the subject of my sentence. And that whole group of words can be regarded as a *noun phrase*.

Notice that I'm using the word "can". This is because I want to stress that grammar is not inflexible. There are different ways of looking at a sentence, just as there are different ways of looking at most things. Some ways of analysing a sentence may be more helpful to you than others. And there are some grey areas, too. This is not an exact science, so try and keep an open mind and think for yourself.

A noun phrase

The reason why I called that group of words a "noun" phrase was because the whole group of words functions like a single noun. This question of function, as I took care to point out early on, cannot be over emphasized. Always try and see how the words are functioning together. If we replace the whole group with the words "My subject", we get the sentence: "My subject is 'Growing Vegetables' ". When we shorten the subject in this way, we can see that it really is a noun group. In more technical language, we could say that "My subject" consists of a noun preceded by a *possessive adjective*. This possessive adjective is also a *personal pronoun*.

In our shortened sentence "My subject is 'Growing Vegetables' ", we have the simple order: subject, the verb "to be", complement. The complement is also a noun phrase. And notice that we say "to be". When we refer to verbs, we have to choose a part which doesn't change. We can't say "the verb 'is' ", because that particular verb is sometimes "was" or "will be" or "are". So we use what is called the *infinitive*, because the infinitive doesn't change. And some people prefer to use the preposition "to" as well, to emphasise the fact. So we talk of the verbs "to sleep", "to walk" and "to smile"; or "sleep", "walk", "smile". We couldn't possibly talk of the verb "slept" because that is only one of the forms of this particular verb.

Our subject, then, could be a single noun, or a noun phrase. It could also be a *noun clause*, and perhaps this is the time to contrast *finite* forms of the verb and the infinitive, although there will be more to say about this in later chapters. The point is that the infinitive really is just that: *non-finite*, or without any kind of time marker. "To sleep" isn't about sleeping today, yesterday, or tomorrow.

Phrases and clauses

Phrases may have verbs, but they are always non-finite, but clauses have to contain finite verbs. Look at these three sentences:

"I was so happy to see my friend."
"Seeing my friend made me so happy."
"I was so happy because I saw my friend."

The first sentence contains the infinitive "to see" and this infinitive introduces the phrase "to see my friend". In the second sentence, the "-ing" form of the verb, which is also non-finite, introduces the phrase "seeing my friend". But in the third sentence, the conjunction "because" introduces a clause which contains the finite verb "saw". Whereas the first two sentences contain only one clause because there is only one finite verb in each ("was" and "made"), the third sentence contains two clauses because there are two finite verbs. The two finite verbs are "was" and "saw". The two clauses are: "I was so happy" and "because I saw my friend".

Building up sentences

The point about single parts of speech, phrases, and clauses, is best shown by building a sentence up from something very simple. Let's take our sentence: "The dog bit the man."

Once again, we can analyse this sentence as: subject (noun), verb (finite), object (noun). We can expand our subject by describing it. We can write "The black dog bit the man." We can expand our sentence even further by describing the object: "The black dog bit the fat man." Because the words "black" and "fat" are descriptive, we call them adjectives. We can further expand these adjectives into adjective clauses by writing: "The dog which was black bit the man who was fat.'' Notice that, this time, we have used two new parts of speech: the words ''which'' and ''who''. We call these *relative pronouns*. They are pronouns because they refer, or relate to, nouns. And these relative pronouns can be used to introduce what is called the *relative clause* or the *adjective clause*. There are two names for this kind of clause, depending on how we see its function. And these two groups of words – ''which was black'' and ''who was fat'' are clauses because they include a finite form of the verb ''to be'', namely ''was''.

We now have the sentence: ''The dog which was black bit the man who was fat.'' We can further expand this sentence by adding an adverb – in this case an *adverb of time*: ''The dog which was black bit the man who was fat, yesterday''. In English, we can put the adverb of time at the beginning, if we like: ''Yesterday, the dog which was big bit the man who was fat''.

By adding an adverbial phrase, we can extend our sentence even further: ''Yesterday, the dog which was big bit the man who was fat on the leg''. Notice that this is a phrase but not a clause, because it does not contain a finite – or any form of a verb, in fact. Notice also that, this time, we cannot move the new adverbial phrase to the beginning of our sentence. English syntax will not allow us to do that.

We can, then, build up sentences with all our parts of speech. And since these parts of speech can be expanded to form phrases and clauses, this is perhaps a good time to look more closely at what these parts of speech are.

Parts of speech

The generally recognised list of parts of speech is as follows: nouns, pronouns, adjectives, adverbs, prepositions, conjunctions, articles, and *determiners*. But it's worth pointing out that there is some debate over their classification and their number. Remember, when you have difficulty over classifying a word into its part of speech – as we all do, from time to time – this is often because of the difficulty of exact description of how the language actually works. It all depends on how we are looking at that bit of language, and what kind of functional *usage* we are concerned with. 'Usage' simply means the way the language is used.

Nouns, then, are the names of persons, places, and things, although some of the things are abstract. In addition to abstract and concrete nouns, we have *proper nouns*, which refer to actual names like "Jack", "Doncaster", "Buckingham Palace". All nouns which are not actual names can be called *common nouns*. Some of the nouns are *countable*, which means that they can be plural (like "bottle/bottles" and "man/men"); but others are *uncountable*, which means that we cannot make them plural (like "milk").

Pronouns

Pronouns are interesting because we can use them instead of nouns. Remember how tedious it was to have to keep mentioning who or what we were writing about all the time? "Mr Smith went into town and then Mr Smith got out of Mr Smith's car, picked up Mr Smith's driving licence, locked Mr Smith's car door, and went into the post office". It was so much easier to write: "Mr Smith went into town and then he got out of his car, picked up his driving licence, locked his car door, and went into the post office".

Pronouns can be divided into the following types: personal and impersonal (which we already know about), relative, *interrogative* (used for questions), and *demonstrative* (used to demonstrate, or point out, a particular thing). The personal pronouns are: "I", "me", "we", "us", "you", "he", "him", "she", "her", "they", "them", and the impersonal pronoun is "it". The relative pronouns are: "who", "whom", "whose", "which", "that". The interrogative pronouns are the same, except for "that". And the demonstratives are: "this", "these", "that", "those".

Once again, it is very important to realise that these classifications are not completely water-tight. But they will do for our purposes and are sound enough to learn and be taught to others. There is a continuous debate on the best way to break down and classify these functional and descriptive elements of languages, and that debate is likely to continue. Indeed, it is well to beware of those who are too insistent and categorical in these matters.

Adverbs and prepositions

Any word which is used for descriptive purposes is likely to be an adjective. In English, they tend to come before nouns.

Adverbs, on the other hand, form a large and complex group. Basically, they can be divided into different types: *adverbs of degree* (answering the question: How much?), *adverbs of duration* (answering the question: How long?), *adverbs of frequency* (answering the question: How often?), *adverbs of place* (answering the question: Where?), and *adverbs of time* (answering the question: When?). Under 'degree', we might list words like: "completely", "almost", "nearly". Under 'duration', we might list words like: "since", "from", "until". Under 'frequency', we might list words like "often", "never", "usually", "sometimes", "always". Under 'place', we might list words like: "down", "across", "over", "beneath". And, under 'time', we might list words like: "again", "tomorrow", "yesterday".

Adverbs and prepositions are easily confused. Sometimes, we just cannot be sure whether a word is best seen as a preposition or as an adverb. When these are expanded into phrases and clauses, there can be further confusion. But we do need to have these terms so that we can better describe what is happening in the language. Generally, it is best to think of prepositions as those short words which tend to come before nouns ('pre-positioned'). We are thinking of words like: "of", "in", "to", "from" and so on. It's not quite as simple as that, but it will do for now.

Conjunctions and articles

Conjunctions join things together, most commonly nouns. Simple examples are: "and" and "but". The articles are divided into *definite* ("the") and *indefinite* ("a", "an", "some"). Articles, like adjectives, can be placed before a noun to modify it in some way. Just as "tall" men are different from "short" men, so "a" man is different from "the" man. There are other words which can be placed before nouns to modify them in some way: words like "all", "these", and "many". For this reason, some grammarians group the articles and these other words into a single category and call them *determiners*.

All these various, and rather complicated and detailed, parts of speech are important as we come to build our sentences. We need such terms if we are, at the very least, to give a reasonable description of what we see when we look at a sentence in English. They are meant to help rather than hinder and, admittedly, they do take rather a lot of digesting. But keep in mind the fact that we cannot properly talk about how we build our sentences up without using such terms.

We shall be returning to and recycling all this in later chapters but, for the time being, here is a revision of the new terms we have met in this chapter:

New Grammatical Terms (5)

adjective clause a clause which is used to describe something and is introduced by a relative pronoun

adverb of degree answers the question 'how much?'

adverb of duration answers the question 'how long?'

adverb of frequency answers the question 'how often?'

adverb of place answers the question 'where?'

adverb of time answers the question 'when'?

common noun a noun which is not the actual name of something

countable something which can be counted

definite specific

demonstrative points out what we are referring to

determiner a word (including the articles) which acts rather like an adjective in modifying the noun in some way: e.g. ''all men'' and ''both men'', as opposed to simply ''men''

finite linked to time

indefinite unspecific

infinitive the non-finite part of the verb

interrogative asking a question

non-finite unlinked to time; timeless

noun clause like a noun phrase, but containing a finite verb

noun phrase a group of words which is used in the same way as a noun

personal pronoun a pronoun which refers to a person

possessive adjective a describing word in the possessive form

proper noun the actual name of something

relative clause a clause introduced by a relative pronoun

relative pronoun pronoun which is used to introduce a relative or adjective clause

uncountable something which cannot be counted

Revision Five

Here are some questions for you to try:

1. How many types of adverb are there?
2. Can you name the types?
3. Name what types these adverbs are: "yesterday" "sometimes" "nearly" "across".
4. What is an infinitive?
5. Write down the infinitive of "walk".
6. What is another name for a relative clause?
7. Give an example of a countable noun.
8. Which two parts of speech are rather closely related and difficult to define?
9. What are the three basic parts of a simple sentence?
10. What is a finite verb?
11. What is the difference between an object and a complement?
12. What is the difference between a phrase and a clause?
13. How many words are there in the shortest sentence?
14. Why are prepositions called by that name?
15. What does the prefix in the term 'pronoun' suggest to you?
16. Are the terms for parts of speech fixed and definite?
17. What must every sentence have, even if only understood?

Key (Revision 5)

1. Five.
2. Degree, duration, frequency, place, time.
3. Time, frequency, degree, place.
4. The fixed, non-finite form of the verb.
5. "To walk".
6. Adjective clause.
7. Any noun which can have "s" on the end for plural.
8. Adverbs and prepositions.
9. Subject, verb, object/complement.
10. A verb which relates to time.
11. A complement only goes with verbs which cannot have objects, like "to be", "to sleep", "to laugh".
12. A clause must have a finite verb.
13. One.
14. Because they come before nouns.
15. 'instead of'.
16. No.
17. A subject and a verb.

6

Expanding the Parts

We are faced with the outside world and meet it with our experience of it and the need to communicate that experience. We are surrounded by things which we wish to name. Not only that: we need to give names to our thoughts and feelings about the world and ourselves. For all this, we need nouns: both concrete and abstract.

But naming is not enough. We need to describe the things around us and describe in more detail the ways in which we feel about ourselves and the outside world. For this, we need adjectives.

This world of things, and thoughts and feelings, is not inert and dead. It is a world of action, in time. Before any of this can begin to happen and move, we need verbs. We need verbs to deal with the past, the present, and the future.

Not only that. We also need to speak of how, when, where, and why these things happen. For all these reasons, locations, occasions in time, we need adverbs. The world of ourselves and our experiences is filled with questions to do with meaning and time. In order to deal with problems, and in order to be more specific about things in general, we need adverbs.

But how to join all these bits and pieces, both large and small, together? For this, we need conjunctions. And, finally, to bind everything up and lock it together, we need a number of very small words – our prepositions – which are rather like tacks or panel pins. They help keep the whole structure together.

It isn't only prepositions, however, that bind our structures together. Sentences are put together in such a way that each linking part fits as seamlessly as possible with its neighbours. It is this apparently seamless linking that gives our sentences the appearance of being watertight and whole. We look at the sentence and have, at first, no way of breaking into it and separating its parts.

The heart of grammatical activity

However, it can be done. And it is this breaking down and building up of sentences which constitutes the heart of grammatical activity. In the old days, it used to be done mechanically and according to the grammar of another language altogether: Latin. Latin is a language which is no longer spoken or written and fitting its grammatical system to English is a hopeless, and senseless, activity. Nowadays, very few would dream of doing so. Instead, we have a new generation of grammarians who are, principally, specialists in linguistics. It is they who have provided the insights which help us lesser mortals to begin to unravel the mysteries of our language.

In this chapter, we are, once again, expanding the parts of our sentence so as to create full and natural language. By that, I mean the kind of language you use when you write letters, diaries, reports, or whatever you use the written form of the language for in your everyday activities. It is that kind of language we are looking at; not some kind of artificial variety. What exists on paper is the real thing. We need not distort it in any way.

Parts of the sentence

To recap. We've learned that any sentence normally has a subject and a verb. That verb can be followed by an object or a complement. A sentence which contains these three basic elements can be very short, of medium length, or very long. In the process of making the sentence longer, we add extra words to its different parts: we can add adjectives to the subject and the object, add adverbs to the verb, and tie the lot together with prepositions. If we wish to join bits together in a fairly basic kind of way, we can use conjunctions.

Let's start with a story

In order to make the building up of sentences more natural, let's imagine we are writing a story of some kind. First of all we need a subject. We'll call our subject, "Mary". But what does she do? "Mary is a cashier." Where? "Mary is a cashier in a bank." What bank? "Mary is a cashier in Wagers bank." Which Wagers bank? "Mary is a cashier in Wagers bank in Wigton." Where is Wigton? "Mary is a cashier in Wagers bank in Wigton, in Brentshire."

We can analyse this sentence by saying that we have written a sentence about Mary. Mary is the subject of our sentence. Mary is a proper noun. Our subject is followed by a form of the verb "to be". Verbs like this are said to be *intransitive*. That is, they are not followed by objects, but by a complement. If a verb can be followed by an object, we call it a *transitive verb*. So we have a subject, a verb, and a complement. To describe the idea of adding to the basic structure of our sentence, I'm going to use the term *adjunct*, although the way I'm using the term isn't strictly orthodox. So, I'm going to say that our complement, "cashier", has been followed by three *adverbials*. I'm going to call the three adjuncts "in Wagers bank in Wigton, in Brentshire" adverbials because, although they begin with prepositions, their function is adverbial: in other words, they answer the question "where?". Remember, many of these terms are inter-changeable, depending on what function we consider the word, phrase, or clause to have, and how we are looking at the whole sentence.

Since we can write a perfectly good sentence if we end at the word "cashier", it is best to regard that as the true complement of our verb. In the case of complements, what comes after the verb belongs to what went before it: Mary equals cashier; cashier equals Mary. All the three adverbial phrases ("in Wagers bank, in Wigton, in Brentshire"), if we take them as a whole, answer the question "where?", so separating them out seems rather false, really.

We could change our sentence slightly and then add more information: "Mary was in Wagers bank in Wigton in Brentshire at ten o'clock on Tuesday when the thieves stormed in." Here, there is little point in talking about complements because our new sentence doesn't point to that kind of analysis. After part of the verb "to be" we have our adverbial group, followed by "at ten o'clock on Tuesday". This is composed of two adverbial phrases which answer the question "when?", so we'll simply call them an adverbial of time. We then have the shorter sentence: "Mary was in Wagers bank in Wigton at ten o'clock on Tuesday." This would make a perfectly good sentence. But we now have something extra added on: "when the thieves broke in." And because this is a group beginning with "when" and containing a finite verb, we can call it an *adverb clause of time*. But it cannot stand on its own: "when the thieves broke in," is not a complete sentence. It could only ever be part of a sentence. If you say it to yourself, you will feel something is missing. It just doesn't make sense.

Because of this, this clause could never be a main clause. It is therefore called a *subordinate clause*. The main clause is "Mary was in Wagers bank in Wigton at ten o'clock on Tuesday". Our new sentence is therefore built up of a main clause and a subordinate adverbial clause. If anyone wrote out the adverbial clause and put a full-stop after it, we could point out that a subordinate clause of this kind can never be regarded as a sentence.

Analysis at different levels

Remember that we can analyse a sentence at several levels. At the level of the word only, we can talk about parts of speech or, as they tend to be called nowadays, *word classes*. In a list of words, "in" and "at" would tend to be classed as prepositions. But note that, once used in sentences, their function is often adverbial. And it is the functional aspect of words or groups of words that we are principally interested in.

Prepositions tend to show relationships between nouns. Positional relationships, for example. The relationship between a book and a table is defined by the preposition: "The book is on the table". If we use the preposition "under" the positional relationship between the two nouns changes. But, taking the whole phrase as one ("on the table"), it is best regarded as an adverbial, answering the question "where?". It all depends on how and at what level we are looking at the words.

If someone wrote "The book is at the table" we would correct the writer by saying that the wrong preposition was being used. If someone wrote "The book is on to the table", we could say that the extra word "to" is not needed in this adverbial, or adverb phrase. The preposition "on" is enough.

Looking at a whole sentence

Let's compose a sentence using all the types of clause, to see what the whole thing looks like, put together.

Here's our sentence: "The man from the tax-office, who says I owe them money, sent me a letter after I had complained about everything."

Just have a look through it and see if you can pick out the following: the noun clause, the adverbial clause, and the relative clause. Remember, the main clause is always a noun clause, the adverbial clause answers a question like "how?" or "when?" or "why?", and the relative clause begins with a relative pronoun. Remember, also, that the clauses which are not the main clause are subordinate clauses.

Right. The main clause is split by the relative clause "who says I owe them money" and is, in fact, "The man from the tax office sent me a letter". The adverbial clause is "after I had complained about everything". Each clause, notice, contains a finite verb: "says", "sent", and "had complained".

It is technically said that adjectives are an example of *modification*. That is, they modify or change the noun in some way. This kind of change can happen before the noun, when it is called *premodification*, and after the noun, when it is called *postmodification*. The phrase "from the tax office" is an example of postmodification: it describes the noun ("man") but comes after it. If we had written "the tax-office man", the adjective "tax-office" would have been an example of premodification. Notice, also, that we would be using a noun as an adjective, because "tax-office" is normally classed as a noun. However, we are interested in the function, rather than the class.

Analysing long sentences
We should not be intimidated by the sheer length of a sentence. Every single sentence in English can be broken down into its larger parts, and those larger parts can be further broken down into smaller phrases and, finally, each word can be assigned to its part of speech, or word class.

Let us consider the sentence I have just written. It contains forty words and therefore qualifies as being rather a long sentence. The first thing we need to do to break the sentence down is to note all the finite verbs. This will give us an idea of how many parts the sentence can initially be broken down into. Here is the full sentence again:

"Every single sentence in English can be broken down into its larger parts, and those larger parts can be further broken down into smaller phrases and, finally, each word can be assigned to its part of speech, or word class."

There are, in fact, only three finite verbs here: "can be broken down", "can be further broken down", and "can be assigned". This means that the sentence has three clauses. We have, in fact, three clauses joined by the conjunction "and". The first clause is: "Every single sentence in English can be broken down into its larger parts". The second clause is: "those larger parts can be further broken down into smaller phrases". The third clause is: "each word can be assigned to its part of speech, or word class". Each clause is a noun clause. The first clause can be regarded as the main clause, and the other two clauses can be regarded as subordinate noun clauses.

Notice, by the way, how the verbs all have three parts.

Verbs are so important in English, and so complicated, that we need to devote quite a lot of our time and thought to them. We'll do this in the next two chapters. For the time being, let's remind ourselves of the technical terms we have come across in this chapter.

New Grammatical Terms (6)

adjunct extra information added to a clause or sentence

adverb clause of time answers the question "when?"

adverbial another term for any kind of adverb, adverb phrase or adverb clause

intransitive verb a verb that is not followed by an object

modification any word or words which modify or change the noun

postmodification occurring after the noun

premodification occurring before the noun

subordinate clause any clause in a sentence which is less important than the main clause and depends on it

transitive verb a verb that is followed by an object

word class another term for 'part of speech'

Revision Six

Try and answer these questions:

1. Name the two ways of modifying a noun.
2. What is the difference between a transitive and an intransitive verb?
3. What is the difference between a main clause and a subordinate clause?
4. What term can be used instead of 'part of speech'?
5. Here is a sentence for you to break up into clauses. Name each subordinate clause and identify the main clause:

   "It wasn't easy to answer all these questions because, although I now know something about grammar, there's still a lot of it which is very confusing."
6. What does a preposition do? Give an example.
7. What do prepositions often function as part of?

Key (Revision 6)

1. Premodification and postmodification.
2. A transitive verb is followed by an object but an intransitive verb is not.
3. A main clause can stand alone as a sentence, but a subordinate clause cannot.
4. Word class.
5. Main clause: "It wasn't easy to answer all these questions".
   Subordinate clause (adverbial): "because there's still a lot of it which is very confusing".
   Subordinate clause (adverbial) "although I now know something about grammar".
   Note: you can, if you like, regard "which is very confusing" as a relative clause and, technically, you should do so because the group contains a finite verb. If you do that, we have three subordinate clauses instead of two.
6. It expresses the relationship between two nouns. "The book is on the table" as opposed to "under" it.
7. Adverbials.

7

The Importance of the Verb

So far, we have been looking at sentences on a more general level. Now, it's time to look at the individual parts of the sentence in much more detail. The first part of the sentence we are going to consider is the verb.

As we learned earlier on, nothing would happen in a language without verbs. Everything would be static. The world of events and thoughts, of time and feelings, would be reduced to lists and exclamations.

At the simplest level, of course, we would be able to get by. Those readers who have spoken a foreign language very badly will be able to recall using sign language and reciting the names of things. "That, please", "Apples?", "Hotel?", "No. Big, please", and so on. It's possible to go further: "Where hotel?" "How much this?", "What time plane?" But on these occasions, we are only leaving out the verb "to be". Leaving out other verbs is not quite so simple.

Another story
Here is a story told without the use of any verbs at all. Can you make sense of it?

"And there this bus, you. A number six. Well, we the bus and upstairs and who you we? Sally Frisby. Yes, Sally Frisby. And you who she with? John Hayes. She. She with John Hayes. You him, you? The bloke who that garage in Wyboston. The one with the green front. Down by the butcher's. Well, when she us she actually. And as for John Hayes, well. He just the other way and his face.''

Here is the story again, with the verbs in their places:

"And there was this bus, you see. A number six. Well, we got on the bus and went upstairs and who do you think we saw? Sally Frisby. Yes, Sally Frisby. And do you know who she was with? John Hayes. She was. She was with John Hayes. You remember him, don't you? The bloke who used to run that garage in Wyboston. The one with the green front. Down by the butcher's. Well, when she saw us she actually blushed. And as for John Hayes, well. He just tried to look the other way and hid his face.''

It may have been possible for you to do without most of those verbs and still get a pretty good idea of what it was all about. But the presence of the verbs makes it so much fuller, clearer, and interesting.

Why verbs are essential
When we want to express complicated thoughts, or deep feelings, verbs are essential. Here is someone trying to explain something complicated but all the verbs have been removed:

"First of all, you the polypin upright and it for about two hours. It a good idea the cap from time to time excess gas. After two hours, the polypin horizontal on a flat surface and again excess pressure. A block of wood about two inches deep and it under the front of the polypin the sediment to the rear of the polypin. After an hour or so, the block of wood carefully under the rear of the polypin the beer easier. The polypin for twenty-four hours in a temperature of about fifty-five degrees Fahrenheit. When you the beer, the tap slowly and the first half pint or so. The beer then clear and ready.''

Here are the instructions in full:

"First of all, you place the polypin upright and leave it for about two hours. It's a good idea to open the cap from time to time to release excess gas. After two hours, place the polypin horizontal on a flat surface and again release excess pressure. Take a block of wood about two inches deep and place it under the front of the polypin to encourage the sediment to sink to the rear of the polypin. After an hour or so, place the block of wood carefully under the rear of the polypin to make the beer easier to serve. Leave the polypin for twenty-four hours in a temperature of about fifty-five degrees Fahrenheit. When you wish to serve the beer, open the tap slowly and drain off the first half pint or so. The beer should then be clear and ready to serve.''

It might have been possible to carry out the operation with only the first set of instructions to go on, but it would have been hazardous and, probably, unsuccessful.

Imagine, then, what it would be like to have to express our deepest feelings without any verbs at all. We might end up having to write something like this:

''I you so much because I you so much. You that. Not a single minute by without my of you. You a nerve in me. Life around me but I always. I of a life with you. I it silly this instead of it to your face, but I you and with you always. One day, I you properly. Who? It next time we.''

The real message behind this frustrating and garbled note was:

''I need you so much because I love you so much. You must understand that. Not a single minute goes by without my thinking of you. You seem to touch a nerve in me. Life goes on around me but I seem to be always dreaming. I dream of a life with you. I know it's silly to write this instead of saying it to your face, but I would love to marry you and live with you always. One day, I will ask you properly. Who knows? It could be next time we meet.''

The verb ''to be'' is, in a sense, the least important of all the verbs. Some languages have no such verb. And, as we saw earlier, it is possible to get along in a foreign language without using it or its equivalent – if there is one. In the same way, people whose native tongue is not English, and who know little of the language, get by well enough without it. We might hear such a person say something like: ''I Polish. I no speak English very well. In Poland, I professor. My wife, she English. We on holiday here.'' There is no problem with this, at all.

However, the verb ''to be'' is so much a part of English

that the language would be clumsy and, in certain cases, impossible without it. It fits seamlessly into the fabric of the language and it also helps us to form complex parts of other verbs. It is used to say things like: "I am going", "I will be seeing John, tomorrow", "I have been ill," and so on.

Here are the parts of the verb "to be" for you to think about:

"am" "is" "are" "was" "were" "being" "been".

Participles

If you try and use these parts of the verb "to be" to make sentences, you will soon meet a few problems. It's easy to make sentences like "I am a teacher. He is a teacher. We are teachers", and go on to say "I was a student. She was a student. We were students." But to use the forms "being" and "been" is rather more difficult. It will be seen that, unlike the other forms, these forms – except for "being" in certain cases – cannot be used alone. For that reason, such forms are referred to as *participles*. They are participles of what is technically referred to as the *copula*. All verbs which link a subject and a complement are called *copular* or *copulative* and the verb "to be" is the significant example of this. The term can be a way of reminding us of this verb's peculiarities.

Without the forms "being" and "been", we would be unable to form very important verb constructions. We wouldn't, for example, be able to say things like "We have been dancing", "The car was being towed", and so on. The language would be terribly poor without such possibilities.

Participles of verbs are divided into only two types: *present participles* and *past participles*. The present participles all end in "-ing", like "speaking", "walking", "thinking". All of these are *regular*. The past participles, however, can be regular or *irregular*. Whereas "walked" is regular, "spoken" and "thought" are irregular.

If you've ever tried to learn French, you will have experienced this problem of irregularity. For students of

English who are not native speakers of the language, these irregular past participles have to be specially learned – or learnt! (If you look in your dictionary under "learn", you will see that both forms of the past participle are possible, and correct. But we can't say "thinked" and "thought": there is only one form.) If we are native speakers of English, it is especially fascinating, and strangely comforting, to remind ourselves that we know so many irregular past participles. This is just one example of how much we really know and how clever we are!

Auxiliary verbs

Another verb which is especially important for forming complex verb constructions is the verb "to have". Like the verb "to be" it can be used as a *helping verb* or, to use the proper technical term, an *auxiliary verb*. Like the verb "to be", it can also be used as a *main verb* – in other words, on its own, with no other verb. We can say "I have two sisters" or "I have a semi-detached house". But we can also say, "I have been sick", where the auxiliary verb "have" is used with the main verb "be". If we said "I have been waiting here for two hours", the auxiliary verbs would be "have" and "be", and the main verb would be "wait".

Notice, by the way, that we can even say things like "He has had his tea", where the verb "have" is used both as an auxiliary and as a main verb together. Once again, it is the function that we are principally interested in.

English uses the auxiliaries to help express notions of time. To express time, we can, of course, use adverbs: words like "yesterday", "tomorrow" and so on. But these alone would be insufficient. We need to express our notions of time in more sophisticated and complex ways.

Future tense

Basically, we have three tenses of the verb: present, past, and future. We say, "I think", "I thought", but when it comes to the future, we need an auxiliary: "I will think" or

"I shall think". In French, for example, we can make the future from our verb by changing its spelling, as we did for the past of "think" to make "thought", but in English we do not have a future form.

The fact that we don't have a future form has led linguists to say that English has no *future tense*. A tense is something we make by putting pronouns in front of our verbs. We can make the *present tense* of "think" by writing "I think, you think, he thinks, she thinks, we think, they think". We can make the *past tense* by writing "I thought, you thought, he thought, she thought, we thought, they thought". But we can't make a future tense in the same way for any of the English verbs.

To make a future tense in English, we have to use three words instead of two. We have to say "I will think, you will think, he will think, she will think, we will think, they will think". We have, in fact, to use an auxiliary.

But what about "shall"? Shouldn't we say "I shall think" instead of "I will think"? And shouldn't we say "we shall think" instead of "we will think"?

If you care to reflect a moment, you will realise that what we usually say is neither "I will" nor "I shall", but "I'll". We call this a *short form*, or more properly a *contraction*. Contractions are much more common in speech than in writing because speech is less *formal*. But whether we use "will" or "shall" in certain cases is a subtle matter, best left for the time being.

Although we do not seem to have a future tense in English – depending on how you see it – we have several interesting ways of expressing the future. We can use what is called the *present simple*, which is the one-word version of the present tense: "We sail tomorrow", for example. This form is used for precise plans – say, military orders.

Other ways of expressing the future are much more common. We can use the *present continuous*, which is the two word version of the present tense. We form it by using a form of the verb "be" and the present participle of the main verb. "We are playing tennis tomorrow", for example. Or we can express the future by using "going to" with the main verb: "We are going to play tennis tomorrow".

In our next chapter, we shall be pursuing this fascinating business of the verb in English in more detail. But for the time being here are our new technical terms and their explanations:

New Grammatical Terms (7)

auxiliary verb the technical term for 'helping verb'

contraction technical term for 'short form' (see below)

copula a verb, commonly "to be", which is followed by a complement

copular the adjective form of the above

copulative another adjective form

future tense the pronoun/verb combinations which express the future

helping verb a verb used to help form a complex verb group

irregular with an uncommon, special form

main verb the form of the verb which can be used without an auxiliary

participle the end part of a verb form, ending in "-ing" or "-ed" (or an irregular past)

past participle a participle which has the ending "-ed" (or an irregular past form)

past tense as above (see 'future tense') for the past

present continuous a form of the present ending in "-ing".

present participle a participle which has the ending "-ing"

present simple the simplest form of the present tense

present tense as above (see 'future tense') for the present

regular with a common form

short form a short combination of two words

Revision Seven

1. What is the copula?
2. What is the present participle of "walk"?
3. What is the past participle of "teach"?
4. Explain three ways of expressing the future.
5. Is the past participle of "run" irregular or regular?
6. What is a contraction?
7. What is more common in speech than "I will"?
8. Give the present simple form of "study".
9. Give the present continuous form of the same verb.
10. What is another name for a helping verb?
11. Explain how "have" can be used as a main verb as well as a helping verb.

Key (Revision 7)

1. The verb "to be" and any verb which is followed by a complement.
2. "walking"
3. "taught"
4. With the auxiliary "will" or "shall", with the present simple, and with "going to". Another way is by using the present continuous.
5. Irregular – because it doesn't end in "-ed".
6. A shortened combination of two separate words, e.g. "it's" for "it is".
7. "I'll".
8. "study/studies"
9. "I am (etc.) studying".
10. An auxiliary verb.
11. We can, for example, write "I have a car" with "have" as a main verb, but also "I have seen the car" where "have" is an auxiliary verb.

8

More About the Verb

Verbs very rarely stand on their own: normally, there is a subject of some kind to which they refer. This subject is either a noun or a pronoun. When verbs do stand alone, they tend to be what are called *imperatives*. Imperatives are commands of some sort: "Stand up!" "Be quiet!" Notice that, even here, the first imperative is followed by an adverbial and the second by an adjective. But although there is no stated subject, the subject is understood as the person, or persons, being addressed.

Because verbs so often have pronouns as their subjects, we tend to consider the pronouns when we talk about verbs and this combination of verb and pronoun is called *conjugation*. However, this term is more properly applied to other highly inflected languages rather than English. The actual spelling of the verb form rarely changes in a particular tense. It changes, for example, in what is called the third *person* of the present tense: with "he", "she", or "it". With the third person, we add an "s": "she speaks".

The persons are divided into six: "I", "you"(singular), "he/she/it", "we", "you" (plural), "they". Each person is classified according to person and number: *first person singular, second person singular, third person singular*, then the change to plural: *first person plural, second person plural, third person plural*. Thus we have "you" as second person singular, and another "you" as second person plural. But, in English, the pronoun has no inflection.

Further divisions of tense

Verbs help us to talk about things in relation to time and, for this purpose, are divided into tenses. As we have seen, the principal divisions are into past, present, and future. But past, present, and future are further divided up into other tenses. We have already met the present simple and the present continuous. There is a *past simple* and a *past continuous* too. An example of the past simple would be "walked" and an example of the past continuous would be "was walking".

Both the present and past continuous are formed by using the verb "be" and the present participle. In the present continuous, the complete present simple of "be" is used to make the tense. Here is the tense in full, using the verb "walk":

I am walking
you are walking
he/she/it is walking
we are walking
you are walking
they are walking

Notice all the pronouns, and notice the changes to the form of the verb "be": "am", "are", "is" and back to "are". The participle stays the same, all the way through.

The past continuous is formed by combining the past simple of the verb "be" and the present participle. Here is the full tense:

I was walking
you were walking
he/she/it was walking
we were walking
you were walking
they were walking

Notice that the pronouns are the same, and notice the changes to the form of the verb "be". Notice, also, that the participle remains unchanged throughout.

If we look at the forms of the verb "be" in both these cases, we can see that in the present simple of the verb there are three different inflections, but in the past simple only two: "was" (for the singular) and "were" (for the plural). In other words, both tenses are partially inflected for both person and number. In some languages, there are full inflections throughout.

We can regard the *future simple* of the verb "be" as this:

I shall/will be
you will be
he/she/it will be
we shall/will be
you will be
they will be

We form the *future continuous* of a verb by, once again, using the present participle but, this time, combining it with the future simple of the verb "be". Thus we have "I shall/will be walking", and so on.

We now have six tenses of the verb: the present simple and the present continuous, the future simple and the future continuous, the past simple and past continuous.

Present and past perfect
The next two important tenses, both concerned with the past, are formed by using the present and past tenses of the verb "have" and the past participle of the main verb.

The first tense we are going to consider is the *present perfect* tense. This is formed by combining the present simple of the verb "have" and the past participle of the main verb. Let's use "walk" again:

I have walked
you have walked
he/she/it has walked
we have walked
you have walked
they have walked

Notice that only the third person singular of the verb "have" changes. Apart from that, there are no changes throughout the tense.

The *past perfect* tense is formed by combining the past simple of the verb "have" with the past participle of the main verb. In this tense, the past simple of the verb "have" remains "had" throughout and there is no change in the past participle. We begin "I had walked" and continue through all persons.

There is another tense which is a further development of the past perfect. This is the *past perfect continuous* tense. The tense is formed by combining the past tense of the verb "have", the past participle of the verb "be" (that is, "been") and the present participle of the main verb. This gives us "I had been walking", for example. Except for the pronouns, there are no changes throughout the tense.

We now have nine tenses: the present simple, the present continuous, the future simple, the future continuous, the past simple, the past continuous, the present perfect, the past perfect, and the past perfect continuous. But it is worth remembering that there is a tendency not to talk about future tenses at all, in which case we would only have seven. And most modern grammarians restrict the total number to eight by including only one more tense: the *present perfect continuous*.

This tense is very similar to the past perfect continuous, except that the present simple of the auxiliary "have" is used instead of the past simple. The first person of the tense is "I have been walking" and, except for the change of pronoun, there is only one other change: in the third person singular, where the "have" changes to "has".

Try not to be intimidated by all this. Remember that you can already handle all this stuff when you speak and write the language. All we are doing, really, is giving labels to what you already know and can use. We are still examining the marvellous richness and versatility of the language. It is something we should be grateful for, rather than diminished by. Anyway, back to our verbs.

What we have been looking at, so far, is how verbs are used to express time (tense) and what is technically called *aspect*. 'Aspect' has to do with whether an action is complete *(perfective)* or continuing (continuous or *progressive*). Indeed, the continuous tenses are commonly called 'progressive', hence the term *present progressive*, for example, instead of 'present continuous'.

But, before we go any further, here is a table of all the tenses, using the verb 'drive':

Present simple	I drive
Present continuous	I am driving
Present perfect	I have driven
Present perfect continuous	I have been driving
Future simple	I shall/will drive
Future continuous	I shall/will be driving
Future perfect	I shall/will have driven
Future perfect continuous	I shall/will have been driving
Past simple	I drove
Past continuous	I was driving
Past perfect	I had driven
Past perfect continuous	I had been driving

The passive form
Up until now, we have been considering the verb in its *active* form, but there is also a *passive* form. When we talk about someone doing something, we use the active form of the verb, but when we talk about something being done by someone, we are using the passive. Technically, we are considering *voice*. Look at the following:

"The dog bit James"

and

"James was bitten by the dog".

The first sentence is active, but the second is passive. The object of the first sentence has become the subject of the second sentence and has been moved to first position. In the process, the verb has become passive. And the passive has been made by using the simple past of the verb "be" and the past participle of the main verb.

There are both past, present, and future passives and we can form passives from all the transitive verbs. We can show this by using the verb "drive" as follows:

Active	Passive
she drives	she is driven
she is driving	she is being driven
she will drive	she will be driven
she will be driving	she will be being driven
she drove	she was driven
she was driving	she was being driven
she has driven	she has been driven
she has been driving	she has been being driven
she had driven	she had been driven
she had been driving	she had been being driven

Notice that we have *passivised* all our ten tenses. We have done this using parts of the verb "be". We have used the simple present, future, and past forms, adding the present participle to the progressives and the past participle to the perfectives.

Some of the verb tenses – and, certainly, many of the passives – are rarely used by many speakers and writers. They are, however, a significant and extremely useful part of the language. Indeed, the flexibility of their *usage* signifies the extent to which we are able to draw on the resources of our language to express complex matters or subtle distinctions. They cannot be ignored.

But we must try not to overwhelm ourselves with the complexity of the verb system in English. Books could be – and have been – written about it. Obviously, we need to be aware of what forms of the verb we need in order to talk about 'time'. We also need to be conscious of how the verb changes to express questions (the interrogative) and *negation* (the *negative*, or forms with "not").

Negatives

Negatives are formed by inserting "not" in various parts of the *verbal group* and using auxiliaries. The "not" has its own fixed place in the order of the verbal group. We say "I am not" but we can't say "I not am". We say "I will not be" but we can't say "I not will be". And so on. With more complex verbal groups, the same applies. We say "By next Friday, I will not have been home for three weeks" and we have to put the "not" before the "have". In the sentence "He has not been examined by a doctor", try putting the negative in different positions and you will see its position is fixed.

Further thought should bring you to see that the negative normally follows the auxiliary verb. In interrogatives, where there is inversion, this is still the case: "Hasn't (has not) he been examined by a doctor?"

The verbal group, active and passive, interrogative and negative, has a fixed order. The grammatical system of the language doesn't allow us to play with it. But our ability to play with the syntax of an English sentence is severely limited anyway. This is because English is relatively *uninflected*. In a highly *inflected* language we know the word class of a word by its inflection: a special ending to show whether it is the subject or object, for example. Where this is not the case, word order becomes far less flexible.

Modal auxiliaries

Our knowledge of the verb is not restricted to main verbs and the auxiliaries "be" and "have". To make negatives and interrogatives in English, we also need the auxiliary "do": "I don't like grammar" and "Do you like it?" for example. But there are other auxiliaries, too: "can", "could", "may", "might", "shall", "should", "will", "would", "must", "ought to", "used to", "need to" and "dare". But these particular verbal auxiliaries are called *modal auxiliaries*. They are called 'modal auxiliaries' because they express what in grammar is called *mood*. This is not a particularly expressive term and the best way to remember it is by remembering the auxiliaries that come within the term.

If we look at the modal auxiliaries, we can see that ideas of possibility, probability, duty, necessity, and habit are being suggested. And this is the best way to think of them. The negative changes, or modifies, the verbal statement in some way. So do the modals. We "might" do this, or we "used to" do this, or we "should" do this.

But these modal auxiliaries are not verbs in their own right. We can't "should" or "might" anybody. They are truly dependent. In a statement like "That letter should have been written yesterday", the auxiliaries are all dependent on the main verb for meaning. Take out "written" and the sense is lost.

The subjunctive

Connected with modal auxiliaries is something called the *subjunctive*, and you will come across talk of the 'subjunctive mood'.

In the sentence "I wouldn't do that if I were you", the form of the verb "be" is unusual. We would expect it to be "was" in this case. The form "were" expresses something which is not a fact but a supposition or condition, and we call this particular form 'the subjunctive'. Notice the word "if", which is a signal of subjunctive use. However, there is a strong tendency nowadays to use the normal form in these situations. "I wouldn't do that if I was you."

The subjunctive is sometimes used after "as if": "He looked at me as if I were mad", but here again there is a modern tendency to use the normal form of the verb. Even with the verb "wish", as when we are imagining something, there is a modern tendency not to use a subjunctive form: "I wish I was in sunny Hawaii rather than in rainy England". It is not for the individual to decide whether the subjunctive be abolished or not, and linguists are beginning to say that the form I've just used is making a comeback due to American influence.

There are two forms of the subjunctive: present and past. With the verb "be", the present subjunctive has only the one form "be". In the past, the form "were" is used.

Verbal groups

Certain verbal groups are generally regarded as complete and separate verbs in their own right. Verbal groups like "put up with" (meaning "tolerate") cannot be broken up. All the parts belong to each other. In the sentence "I put up with him for too long" we cannot break up "put up with" by inserting "him" between any of the words in the verbal group. We can't say "I put him up with for too long", for instance.

We have to distinguish between these verbal groups and verbs which do not belong to an identifiable verbal group. You can "put up the curtains" and "put the curtains up". And this suggests that we have here a verbal group "put up" which is properly considered as a *two-word verb*. Because the grammar of these kinds of verbs is so complex, we often prefer to talk of *multi-word verbs*. This avoids the problem of coping with other, more descriptive, definitions.

There is an easily identifiable group of verbs which consist of a verb and an adverb, and which are intransitive. Verbs like "get by", "turn up", and "take off". These can be used in sentences like: "I haven't got much money, but I get by", "He turned up at two o'clock", and "When does the plane take off?" We can't split these two-word verbs up.

Other verbs which contain the same words behave in a different way. Consider the sentences: "I turned up my skirt", "Take off those wet things". These verbs are all transitive and we can put the object after the main part of the verb: "I turned my skirt up", for example. The bit on the end of the verb, by the way ("up", in this case), is called a *particle*.

Although the grammar of such verbs is far too complex to consider here, it is important to see the difference between a typical multi-word verb and a verb followed by a preposition. Here are some normal examples of a verb followed by a preposition: "He walked up the street", "He turned into the driveway", "The little girl took her shoes off the table". In all these cases, the object cannot be placed in front of the preposition. We can't say: "He walked the street up".

We shall be looking more closely at verbal groups in Chapter 11, but that's enough of the verb for the time being. It's now time to review the terms we have come across in this chapter:

New Grammatical Terms (8)

active direct action by the subject

aspect the way a verb expresses 'time'

conjugation the way a verb is combined with its pronouns

first person plural "we"

first person singular "I"

future continuous "I shall/will be walking" etc

future simple "I shall/will walk" etc

imperative a form of the verb which expresses a command

inflected with inflection

modal auxiliary the auxiliary through which the mood is expressed ("may", "should" etc)

mood the verbal expression of attitude

multi-word verb a verb consisting of two or more words

negation using "not"

negative the actual form with "not"

particle the word or words added to a single-word verb to make it a multi-word verb

passive where the subject is being acted upon

passivise to make an active sentence passive

past continuous "I was walking" etc

past perfect "I had walked"

past perfect continuous "I had been walking"

past simple "I walked" etc

perfective finished action

persons what pronouns are called in a verbal combination

present perfect "I have walked" etc

present perfect continuous "I have been walking"

present progressive another name for the present continuous

progressive continuing action

second person plural "you"

second person singular "you"

subjunctive the use of a special form of the verb to express hypothesis, supposition, or condition. It is quite common after "if" and "whether". There are two forms: present ("be") and past ("were")

third person plural "they"

third person singular "he/she/it"

two-word verb a verb of two words only

uninflected without inflection
usage the way language is used
verbal group a term for the verb phrase
voice the active or passive mode

Revision Eight

Here are some questions for you to try:

1. How many persons are there in a verb conjugation?
2. What is another name for the 'continuous'?
3. What are the names of the continuous tenses?
4. Give two examples of a perfective.
5. What form of the verb do we use to give commands?
6. What is 'aspect'?
7. Is this sentence active or passive: "John finished his essay on time"?
8. Passivise this sentence: "The cat ate all the meat".
9. What term is used to cover the notions of active and passive?
10. What is 'usage'?
11. What is another name for the verb phrase?
12. Give three examples of modal auxiliaries.
13. What is a particle?

Key (Revision 8)
1. Six.
2. The 'progressive'.
3. Present continuous, future continuous, past continuous, present perfect continuous, future perfect continuous, past perfect continuous.
4. "I have walked" and "I had walked".
5. The imperative.
6. The way the verb is used to express 'time'.
7. Active.
8. "All the meat was eaten by the cat."
9. 'Voice'.
10. The way the language is used.
11. The verbal group.
12. Any of the following: "can" "could" "may" "might" "shall" "should" "will" "would" "must" "ought to" "used to" "need" "dare".
13. The second or third part of a multi-word verb.

9

Adjectives and Description

Although, as we already know, it is possible to write sentences without adjectives, we need them to give more life to what we write. The world around us begs to be described, as do our feelings.

Other people are always asking us what things are like: "What was your holiday like?", "What's your boyfriend like?", "What's your new car like?". It's difficult to answer questions like these without using adjectives.

We know that, in English, adjectives normally come before nouns. That is their simplest occurrence. We talk and write about "big houses", "smart suits", "smooth lawns", and so on. But adjectives can be part of far more complex constructions than that. As well as premodifying nouns, when they have what is called an *attributive* function, they can also postmodify nouns. In the sentence "The house is big", the adjective follows the noun, rather than coming before it. In the example, the adjective "big" is termed a *subject complement* and, because it occurs in the predicate, the adjective is said to have a *predicative* function.

Of course, the adjective itself can be premodified. We can, for example, put what is called an *intensifier* in front of it. We can say that the house is "very big" instead of just "big".

Comparatives and superlatives
We often want to do more than simply use an adjective to

describe a noun. Sometimes, we want to make comparisons. We want to use the *comparative* form of the adjective and say that this house is "bigger" than that one. And there are not only *comparative adjectives*, there are *superlative adjectives* as well. This is, perhaps, the "biggest" house in the district.

The various forms of the comparative and superlative can be a problem. We can use an inflection "-er" to show the comparative, and another inflection "-est" to show the superlative. But sometimes this isn't possible. In such cases, we use "more" for the comparative and "most" for the superlative. "More" and "most" tend to be used with longer adjectives. If we made a comparison between the cost of two houses, we might say that the first was "cheaper" than the second, and that the second was "more expensive" than the first. English doesn't like long comparative adjectives. With adjectives of one syllable, the comparative consists of only one word: "larger", "smaller", "richer", "poorer", and so on. But when the adjective consists of two syllables, the language tends to prefer two words rather than one. So we have "more tiring" rather than "tiringer".

But there are some two-syllabled adjectives which can be used either with "more" and "most" or without. "Quiet" and "common" for example. We can say that "Mark is quieter than Richard" or that he is "more quiet" than Richard. When an adjective ends in "-y" we use the inflections rather than "more" and "most". We say that "Richard is happier than Mark", instead of "Richard is more happy than Mark."

However, we mustn't be too dogmatic about all this. Unless an adjective is longer than two syllables – like "inquisitive", "beautiful", "sensible", and so on – there will often be some debate about whether to use an inflected adjective or two words. And here, as in so many areas, the language is gradually changing and developing.

When we want to make a comparison between two things which are equal in some way rather than being different, we can use "as . . . . as". We can say that one house is "as big as" another house. Notice that when we use the comparative adjective, we follow it by the word "than". But what *is* this word "than"? What part of speech, or word class, is it? And what about "as"?

Our answer to such questions really depends on how we are looking at the language, or at what level we are analysing it. When we say that "My house is bigger than your house" or "My house is as big as your house", we are making comparisons, using comparative adjectives. But we are also relating one house to another. If we write "My house is big your house", we are not making a comparison at all. If we write "My house is bigger your house", we are now making a comparison but not in the way the structure of the language demands. Some languages can even omit the verb "be" and say "My house bigger your house". But English needs not only the copulative, but the word "than" as well. The word "than" is an important structural element in the sentence. It is, in addition, interesting to note that "My house is big your house" could be interpreted as either a comparative statement or a superlative statement.

To make a grammatically correct comparison, we must either use an inflected adjective with "than" or an uninflected adjective preceded and followed by "as". The words "as" and "than" gain their significance and meaning from the phrases they belong to. It seems pointless to try to assign them to a particular word class. Rather than do that, it is preferable to regard the group of words that make the comparative as adjectival phrases. At the same time, it is as well to notice that the comparatives show a relationship between two nouns or noun groups.

The – ing form

One of the most interesting forms of adjectives is when they appear to be present participles. When this happens, only a functional approach to the problem will help us sort out which is which. A rigid definition which regards all words which end in "-ing" as being present participles of verbs is particularly unhelpful. There is a profound difference in meaning between "John is thinking" and "John is a thinking person'' and ''Thinking is good for you.'' Only the first ''-ing'' form is truly verbal.

There is, once you begin to consider it, a huge fund of these adjectives which end in ''-ing''. To call them *participial adjectives* is useful, since it shows that their form has a verbal source, but we must not let this detract from the fact that they are true adjectives. We use them in exactly the same way as we do other adjectives. We call these adjectives 'participial' because some are formed from the past participle of verbs. We talk about ''a frightened little girl'', ''a lost cause'', and ''broken windows'', to give just three examples.

Whether we tell someone that ''a conservatory window is broken'' or ''there is a broken window in the conservatory'', the word ''broken'' is an adjective. But when we say that ''someone has broken a conservatory window'', the word ''broken'' is a past participle, and part of the present perfect tense. We have moved from describing a window to talking about what someone has done.

Adjectives and adverbs

Sometimes, adjectives look very like adverbs. The words ''daily'', ''early'', and ''kindly'' look like adverbs because they end in ''-ly'', which is a common adverbial ending. Indeed, all three *can* be adverbs, as in the sentences ''The milkman comes daily'', ''I get up early'', and ''Will you kindly stop smoking?'' We know they are adverbs because they modify the verb ''comes'', ''get up'', and ''stop''. But in sentences like ''The early bird catches the worm'', ''The daily paper always comes late'', and ''It was such a kindly thing to do,'' we can immediately recognise the descriptive function of the ''-ly'' words. They all describe nouns and they must all, therefore, be adjectives.

There are other adjectives which have the same form as adverbs but which do not end in ''-ly''. ''Fast'' for instance, as in ''He drives fast'' and ''He is a fast driver''. In the first sentence, the adverb ''fast'' modifies the verb ''drives''. In the second sentence, the adjective ''fast'' modifies the noun ''driver''.

Adjectives and nouns

We have seen that adjectives are commonly premodifiers of nouns. Nouns, too, can premodify other nouns. However, such nouns, although they have an adjectival function, are not classed as true adjectives because the syntactic arrangements into which they can enter are much more restricted. When we compare, say, "police station" with "pretty station", we can say "The station is prettier this year" or "The station is pretty", but we cannot say "The station is policer this year" or "The station is police". So such nouns are best regarded as part of *compound nouns*, or nouns made up from more than one noun. Whether we join such nouns together to make one word, leave them separate, or *hyphenate* them is another matter.

There are, however, nouns which can function as true adjectives, and vice-versa. A good example is the word "black". Nowadays, it is common, though rather careless and vague, to describe people as "blacks" and "whites" and "coloureds", but people persist in doing so. People talk about "a black", or "a white", or "a coloured", to designate a particular person. But, at the same time, in the singular and without articles, these words are extremely common adjectives. Indeed, it is better to regard their origin as being adjectival rather than *nominal*.

Adjectival phrases and clauses

We must not become too restricted in our consideration of adjectives. When we are thinking about ways of describing the world around us, our feelings, or whatever else it is that we use language to describe, we must remember that we have more than individual adjectives at our disposal. We have not only extremely varied syntactical arrangements, or structures, into which to place our individual adjectives: we have adjectival phrases and clauses which are also at our disposal.

Look at these sentences:

(a) "His house is big."
(b) "My big house is the biggest."

(c) "My house is bigger than his."
(d) "His house is as big as my friend's."
(e) "His house, which is smaller than mine, is as big as my friend's."
(f) "Though smaller than mine, his house is as big as my friend's."
(g) "I find their houses small."
(h) "The fact that their houses are smaller than mine is obvious."

In all these combinations, we have the adjectives "big" and "small" used in different ways. We can describe these different usages in the terminology which we now have available.

(a) "big" used predicatively, as part of the complement
(b) "big" used attributively, as part of the subject, followed by the superlative form used predicatively
(c) "big" used in the comparative form, predicatively, as part of the complement
(d) "big" used as above to show equivalence
(e) "small" used as part of a relative clause followed by the comparative of "big" used predicatively as part of the complement to show equivalence
(f) the comparative of "small" used as part of a subordinate adverbial phrase, followed by the comparative of "big" as part of the main clause and showing equivalence
(g) "small" used predicatively, modifying the object "their houses"
(h) the comparative of "small" as part of a large nominal subject group

But, of course, there are other ways of describing the use of these two adjectives in these sentences. It very much depends on what we are focusing on. And we should never lose sight of the fact that our terminology is there for a purpose. We are trying to describe something complex and, without the use of terminology, such a description would become impossible. How far we decide to take things depends very much on what we are about. If we were explaining things to small children, we should put things in a much simpler way. In fact, there seems little point in introducing difficult terms before they become really necessary.

Whatever we do, we mustn't lose confidence in our ability to acquire the terms and use them. Without the terms, real understanding is not possible. And, once we begin to understand, then we can decide how far we want to take the whole business. Hopefully, gradual confidence building and increasing confidence should lead to the desire to know more about this fascinating subject.

For the time being, here are the new terms followed, as usual, by a short explanation.

New Grammatical Terms (9)

attributive modifying the subject part of the sentence

comparative a word which is used to compare two things

comparative adjective an adjective used to compare two things

compound noun a noun formed from two or more words

intensifier a word which makes another word stronger

nominal to do with the noun

participial adjective an adjective which has the same form as a verb participle

predicative modifying the predicate of a sentence

subject complement referring back to the subject

superlative adjective an adjective used to state that, in a comparison, one element is an extreme example, as in "best" or "worst"

Revision Nine

1. What is the difference between premodification and postmodification?
2. In the sentence "My elder brother is an engineer" why do we say that "elder" is 'attributive'?
3. In the sentence "My sister is a qualified nurse" how would you describe the adjective "qualified"?
4. And how would you describe the phrase "a qualified nurse"?
5. What is an 'intensifier'?
6. When linguists talk of a 'nominal group', what do you think they mean?
7. What are the comparatives of the adjective "wide" and the adjective "sensitive"?
8. What is a participial adjective? How many types are there, and what participles do they originate from?
9. What is a compound noun?
10. How would you describe "as . . . . as"?

Key (Revision 9)

1. Premodification occurs before the noun and post-modification occurs after it.
2. Because in this case the adjective is premodifying the subject of the sentence.
3. The adjective is predicative, because it modifies the predicate of the sentence.
4. This is termed 'the subject complement'.
5. An intensifier is a word like "very" which makes the word it modifies stronger, or more intense.
6. They mean a group of words which combine to create the equivalent of a noun.
7. "wide" "wider" "widest"
   "sensitive" "more sensitive" "most sensitive"
8. An adjective like "sleeping" which is exactly like a verb participle. These adjectives originate from the present participle, which ends in "-ing" and the past participle, which ends in "-ed" when it is regular.
9. A noun made up from two or more words.
10. As the basis for constructing a comparative adjective showing equivalence. The whole construction (e.g. "as tall as") would be called an adjectival phrase.

10

How Adverbs Can Help

Adverbs, as has been said before, are by their very name related to verbs. It's just as well to keep that fact always in mind. Whereas adjectives are closely related to nouns – either alone or in whatever word groups they are dominant – adverbs are always closely associated with those words which activate the sentence and give it life.

Try and see a sentence in your mind's eye. Imagine its subject, there at the beginning, inert but waiting to be brought into an action or event of some kind. Imagine, if you like, the totality of that subject, with its accompanying modifying adjectival element. However short and simple or long and complicated that subject is, it remains inert and unrelated to anything until a transitive verb is introduced. Once that has been done, the world gets into motion again. Things happen.

As your sentence develops, the transitive verb you introduced allows your subject to do something. It allows your subject to affect an object of some kind, which forms round another simple or complex nominal group. Once that has been done, your sentence is complete.

In a rich and complex sentence with a transitive main verb, we would expect not only nouns, adjectives, and verbs to be present, but the other word classes as well. There would be prepositions and conjunctions that bind our sentence together and are called, for that reason, *structural words*. On their own, structural words like ''in'', ''at'', ''and'', ''but'', and so on, appear to convey no meaning.

But they tie everything up into a whole.

Outside all these nouns, adjectives, verbs, prepositions, and conjunctions, is the class of words we call 'adverbs'. And although, as we have already said, such words are closely related to verbs, this class is probably the most problematic of the word classes. The reason for this is that, whereas it is relatively easy to identify nouns, adjectives, prepositions and, to a lesser extent perhaps, conjunctions, the identification of adverbs is often not so easy. Why is this?

Traditional grammar tended to show quite clearly how adverbs related to verbs. Something happened, for example, and the adverb expressed how, why, when, or where it happened. For various reasons, modern grammarians have decided that restricting adverbs to these clear and specific functions fails to account for what really happens in sentences.

A good starting-point

In discussing adverbs, we shall have to consider some of these matters but, for the time being, the traditional definition of adverbs and how they function in sentences is a good starting point.

In traditional grammar, adverbs modify the verb by telling us how, where, when, and how often an action happened. Adverbs which tell us how someone did something are called *adverbs of manner*. Adverbs which tell us where someone did something are called *adverbs of place*. Adverbs which tell us when someone did something are called *adverbs of time*. And adverbs which tell us how often someone did something are called *adverbs of frequency*. These are the four main categories of adverb.

"Cautiously", "angrily", "gently", are examples of adverbs of manner. "Outside", "nearby", "aloft", are examples of adverbs of place. "Yesterday", "tomorrow", "tonight", are adverbs of time. "Never", "sometimes", and "usually", are examples of adverbs of frequency.

If you take a pencil and a piece of paper and try to add

adverbs in these four categories, you will soon find your mind drying up. The reason for this is that when we want to say how, where, when, and how often something is done, we tend to think in groups of words rather than in single adverbs. We tend to say things like "My auntie Bessy behaved in a very funny way the day before yesterday". Or "It's in the bottom left hand drawer". Or "She always comes to see me on the second Friday of every month". Because of this, we prefer to talk of adverbials rather than adverbs. This allows us the freedom to group words together when they obviously function in an adverbial way. We can still keep our four main categories, but we can add further adverbials to them: adverbials like "on all fours", "not far from", "the day before", and "once or twice a week".

Once we have extended our notion of the adverb in this way, the construction of sentences which contain adverbials is relatively easy. Here are four simple examples:

1. "He came charging round the corner without thinking."
2. "She has a nice little place right next to the butcher's shop."
3. "See you at the usual time."
4. "She comes round once or twice a week."

The third sentence above can serve to highlight the problem of when and where to call a particular group of words 'prepositional' or 'adverbial'. The word "at" appears automatically to belong to the word class which includes words like "by", "with", "to", or "from", all of which are normally regarded as prepositions. In that sense, the phrase "at the usual time" can rightly be called a prepositional phrase. A prepositional phrase is simply a phrase which begins with a preposition. But beyond reminding us of the fact that there are a large number of such prepositional phrases in English, such a definition does little to describe the structure of our sentence.

What we are concerned with here is the function of the group of words. In this case, the function of our group is to say when the speaker of the sentence promises to see the other person. We mustn't be too literal with our analysis. After all, we don't regard the verb "see" here in its common sense of using our sight, any more than we regard it as an imperative of the verb. We correctly interpret "see you" as meaning "I'll meet you again".

Maybe now we can begin a loosening-up process in relation to adverbs, since doing so will open up important aspects of grammatical analysis.

We have already considered the way in which adverbs modify verbs, although this is not a modern way of describing what happens. Modern grammarians are more interested in other kinds of adverbial modification, such as the modification of adjectives, other adverbs, prepositions, and even nouns. Let us take each of these in turn.

Adverbial modification

Sometimes we need to say more than that "John is a tall man": we want to say more about his height. Is he "very tall"? "quite tall"? or perhaps "extraordinarily tall"? In order to describe more fully John's tallness – to coin a new word – we use the adverbs "very", "quite", and "extraordinarily". These adverbs are modifying the adjective "tall" in each case.

Incidentally, the majority of adverbs are formed from adjectives, usually by adding "-ly" to the adjectives. The adverb "extraordinarily", formed from the adjective "extraordinary", is just one example. No doubt, you can think of many others.

Just as we often want to describe something more fully by modifying our adjectives, so we often want to say more about *how* things are done. In other words we want to modify our adverbs. We can say that "John is very tall", but we can also say that "John eats very quickly", where the adverb "quickly" is being modified by another adverb "very".

When we say that "John kicked the ball straight into the hall", the adverb "straight", in addition to describing how John "kicked" the ball, also describes how it went "into

101

the hall". Rather than bouncing about, or going up and coming down again, it went "straight into" the hall. So, in this case, we can talk about the adverb modifying the preposition "into".

If we reworded our sentence and said that "John kicked the ball straight into the upstairs bedroom", we could say that the adverb "upstairs" modifies the noun "bedroom". "Upstairs" is an adverb of place. If we said "the bedroom upstairs", then the adverb "upstairs" would be an example of postmodification rather than premodification.

Certain adverbs – like "above" and "below" – can be used both as adverbs and as prepositions. In the sentence "The room above is below the attic", "above" is an adverb modifying the noun "room", but "below" is a preposition. Notice that adverbs often stand alone, whereas prepositions are normally, by definition, 'pre-positioned', or 'put in front of', a noun. But this is a very difficult area of grammar, and so much depends, as it usually does, on how you are analysing the sentence itself.

Perhaps the best transition from the idea of single word adverbs to a consideration of groups of words, which have an adverbial function and are better called 'adverbials', is via the idea of traditional adverb clauses.

We can expand our primary division of adverbs into *adverb clauses of manner*, *adverb clauses of time*, *adverb clauses of place*, and *adverb clauses of frequency*. We can add *adverb clauses of condition*, *adverb clauses of reason*, and *adverb clauses of result*.

Each of these seven clauses will tend to express the seven ideas. Here are examples of each of the seven categories, with the clause highlighted:

"She acted *as though she owned the place.*"
"I'll see you *when you get back from holiday.*"
"You didn't tell me the place *where we were going to have the meeting.*"
"I see him *whenever I get the chance.*"
"I'll tell you my secret *if you tell me yours.*"
"I left *because I didn't like the job.*"
"He didn't work *so he didn't pass.*"

Remember that we call these groups of words 'clauses' because they are like miniature sentences although, unlike sentences, they cannot stand alone. If we express the same ideas, without using main verbs, we end up with adverb phrases of the same types. Here are examples:

"She acted *like the boss*."
"I'll see you *on your return*."
"You didn't tell me the place *for the meeting*."
"I see him *at every opportunity*."
"I'll tell you my secret *in return for yours*."
"I left *because of the job*."
"He didn't work, *hence the failure*.

By treating our description of these groups of words semantically, we can better appreciate the way that groups of words, called clauses or phrases, can behave like single adverbs. A further step is to move away from the idea of single adverbs and to speak rather of 'adverbials'. This allows us to see adverbial functions operating within our sentences, irrespective of whether we are talking of single words or groups.

Flexibility of position
One of the interesting things about these adverbials is their flexibility of position. In the examples above, four of the adverbials can be placed at the beginning of the sentence, or in *initial position*, or at the end of the sentence, in *end position*. In the sentences below, we see an adverbial in initial, *medial*, and end position:

"*On Tuesday*, I'm going to see my dentist."
"I'm going, *on Tuesday*, to see my dentist."
"I'm going to see my dentist *on Tuesday*."

Because they are often what we might call 'add-ons', adverbials are commonly considered as adjuncts. In the three sentences above, the removal of the adverbial still leaves a perfectly comprehensible sentence: "I'm going to see my dentist''. This idea of adjuncts is particularly useful when considering all those little adverbials which find their way into so many different parts of sentences.

At first, these adverbials look so different from our traditional definitions of what an adverb is. They seem to have nothing to do with time, place, manner, or whatever. Rather, they seem like afterthoughts, or little words empty of meaning – rather like prepositions, perhaps. I'm thinking of single word adverbials like "certainly", "really", "perhaps", and multi-word adverbials like "in fact" and "of course". Again, the interesting thing about these adverbials is their free-positioning characteristic. We can put them almost anywhere:

"Of course, he's married now."
"He is, of course, married now."
"He's married now, of course."
"He, of course, is married now."
"He's married, of course, now."

The distinction between adverbs and adverbials, and the division into types, is by no means definite and decided. We have here an area of the grammar which is constantly being revised and expanded, and this is likely to continue. One of the areas where problems come into sharp focus is when considering adverbs which are parts of verbs like "brush up", as in "brush up your grammar".

Adverb or preposition?

In "brush up your grammar", the word "up" looks very much like a preposition but its grammar is more limited than that of a true preposition. In the sentence "He brushed up his grammar" the word "up" expresses the relationship between a pronoun and a noun, which is exactly what a preposition does. We could compare the sentence: "He looked up the chimney." But we can also say "He brushed his grammar up" and this suggests that the word "up" is not functioning as a preposition. We could never say, "He looked the chimney up".

If we say to someone "Look up!", the word "up" is obviously an adverb, as it is in "Look down!" But when we say "Look up the chimney", the word "up" is functioning as a preposition. The thing to notice is the way the preposition clings closely to the noun it precedes. Adverbs, on the other hand, relate closely to verbs.

All this suggests a close relationship between our verb "brush" and its particle "up" which is stronger than any prepositional relationship with a verb would be. "Brush up" asks to be taken as a whole rather than two separate elements.

What about three-word verbs, like "put up with"? In the sentence "Sally couldn't put up with Tom any longer", what is the function of "up" and "with"? If we translate the sentence as "Sally couldn't tolerate Tom any longer", we see the equivalence between the two verbs ("put up with" and "tolerate") very clearly. But we also notice that the two particles have no separate grammatical function.

In grammar, it is most important to concentrate on the function of the word we are looking at. Where the word appears to have no obvious grammatical function, there is little point in debating whether it is a preposition or an adverb.

Exploring a longer sentence

Let's explore a long sentence and see if we can isolate what is adverbial in it. Here is the sentence:

"As a result, George, who is a good friend of mine and who usually comes with me on long journeys, decided, in fact, to do otherwise, simply because he didn't feel in a very good mood that day."

The essential statement in the sentence is that George decided not to travel on the long journey with his friend. He decided to do "otherwise". "Otherwise" is an adverb meaning "differently". The word "simply" is another adverbial, and modifies the word "because". The word "because" itself is not regarded as an adverbial, even if it does normally introduce an adverbial phrase or clause. It is, in fact, regarded as a conjunction, because it is used to link a subordinate clause to preceding parts of the sentence. "As a result" and "that day" are adverbials of result or consequence and time respectively, and the phrase "in fact", although adverbial, could also be regarded as an adjunct. Finally, we have the word "usually", which is an adverb of frequency.

So, then, with a little practice, we can begin to appreciate the nature of adverbials, but it takes time. In a way, our lack of certainty over the adverbial element in a sentence is a good thing. As I've said before, professional grammarians are themselves often at loggerheads over their best definition. The reason for the uncertainty is because the traditional definition of an adverb was far too limited. When it came to exploring the structure of sentences in greater depth, the inadequacy of the term led to differences in terminology as well as conflicting analyses. This shouldn't surprise us. The more one discovers about language, the more there is still to discover. For readers of this book, the more traditional descriptions I've used here should be satisfactory. But, hopefully, there will be others who will want to go much further into the subject.

But let's review our new terms. You will be pleased, by the way, to notice that the list is much simpler than previously. Here is the new list:

New Grammatical Terms (10)

adverb clause of condition a clause, normally beginning with 'if', which expresses condition

adverb clause of frequency a clause which has the same function as the single adverb of frequency

adverb clause of manner a clause which has the same function as the single adverb of manner

adverb clause of place a clause which has the same function as the single adverb of place

adverb clause of reason a clause which tells us why something is or was so

adverb clause of result a clause which, normally beginning with "so" or "therefore", expresses result

adverb clause of time a clause which tells us when something is done

adverbs of manner adverbs which tell us how something is or was done

end position at the end of a string of words

initial position at the beginning of a string of words

medial position in the middle of a string of words

structural words words that bind sentences together but have no special meaning in isolation

Revision Ten

1. Why has the term 'adverb' been traditionally used?
2. What are the traditionally recognised four main types of adverb?
3. Why would you use the term 'adverbial' in preference to the term 'adverb'?
4. How many types of adverbial clause do you know of? What are they?
5. Do adverbs, adverbial phrases, and adverbial clauses have the same function?
6. What is an adjunct? Give an example.
7. What ending do adverbs commonly have?
8. Give three examples of structural words. Why do they have this name?
9. In the sentence "He was simply wonderful", what is the word "simply" doing?
10. What is the full term for this function?
11. Would you call our description of adverbs 'structural' or 'semantic'?
12. In the command "Look it up", would you call "up" a preposition or an adverb?
13. In the command "Look up the chimney!" would you call "up" a preposition or an adverb?
14. Would you say that the grammar of adverbs is fixed and decided or would you say that this is an area of much debate?
15. How final is grammatical terminology?

Key (Revision 10)

1. Simply because it suggests the idea of adding to the verb.
2. Manner, time, place, and frequency.
3. Because it can refer not only to single adverbs but also groups of words with an adverbial function.
4. Seven. Manner, time, place, frequency, condition, reason, and result.
5. Yes, they do.
6. A word or phrase which is added on to a sentence as an extra, but the sentence is in no way dependent on it. Examples are: "occasionally", "of course", "indeed".
7. Normally "-ly".
8. "in" "of" "at". Because they bind together different groups of words but have no intrinsic meaning.
9. Modifying "wonderful".
10. Premodification.
11. Semantic, really, because it relies very much on our understanding of the meaning of sentences.
12. An adverb.
13. A preposition.
14. Certainly not fixed. This is an area where there are many different approaches and descriptions.
15. Much of the terminology is far from final, and new descriptive terminology is being introduced as new linguistic research is published.

11

Tying Things Together: Prepositions

If English sentences were deprived of prepositions, they would look something like this: "I went the chemist's and asked a toothbrush. The shop assistant looked the shelves and found one. She put it a bag. When I put my hand my purse, there was no money it. 'I must have left my money home,' I said. The shop assistant laughed. 'I'll keep it you,' she said. So I went the shop and got my car. I had to drive all the traffic to reach my house, which is the outskirts. It took me an hour to get back the shop."

The missing prepositions are: "to", "for", "on", "in", "at", "out of", "into", "through". If you study each of these prepositions you will probably come to the conclusion — and rightly so — that they are more than just structural words. They do more than simply hold, or bind, words and groups of words together. For this reason, modern grammarians are reluctant to talk about words that are empty of meaning.

It is not difficult to imagine motion "to" things, things being "on" other things, things being "in" other things, things being "at" a certain place, and so on. We imagine "in-ness", "on-ness", "at-ness", "through-ness", without much difficulty.

Positional relationships in space
But it is far easier to think of these words in relation to other things. Indeed, almost all the prepositions can

express positional relationships in space. If you look around you as you read this, and consider where everything in the room is, you will almost certainly be forced to make relationships between the things in the room. Each thing has a position in relation to another thing. In describing that relationship, we need prepositions.

As we look around, we see that the clock is "on" the wall, the mug is "on" the table, the cat is "in" the chair, the books are "on" the shelves, the dictionary is "beside" the chair, the computer is "between" the bookshelves and the cupboard.

And things move. The cat goes "out" of the room, a car drives "past" the window, you take a book "from" the shelves, a spider walks "along" the window sill, a fly flies "around" the room, a plane goes "over" the house, and so on.

In this sense, the recognition of prepositions isn't difficult. We soon get the idea of how they work. In our statements, we notice a relationship between one thing – or noun – and another. We notice a relationship between a clock and a wall, a book and some shelves, a dictionary and a chair.

Prepositions turning into adverbs
When the second party to the relationship disappears, prepositions turn into adverbs. So adverbs often come at the end of short statements. Some prepositions can actually change: "in" can change to "inside", for instance. Others can be used as prepositions without changing: "above", "before", "below", and so on.

When we say "The cat is inside", the word "inside" is an adverb. Or so it seems. It tells us where the cat is, as in "the cat's here". The word "here" is an adverb of place. But the odd thing is that although we can't relate "here" to a following noun, we can "inside". We can say "the cat is inside the house", in which case "inside" becomes, by definition, a preposition. It is placed before the noun "house" and expresses a relationship between "cat" and "house". We could get over this problem by calling

111

"inside" a prepositional adverb.

But that, to me, seems to confuse the issue. There seems little point in creating a category only to obscure it. I prefer to think of certain words as belonging to a particular word class in different functional situations. Words which predominantly belong to one word class sometimes behave as if they belonged to another. However, it is the predominant word class that we should focus on.

So far, we have mentioned the following prepositions: "to", "for", "on", "in", "at", "out of", "into", "through", "past", "from", "along", "around", "over". We shall regard "inside" and "outside" as adverbs of place. And although "on", "in", "through", "past", "along", "around", and "over" can be used adverbially, we shall regard them as basically prepositions. We do, I think, normally think of them as being words which establish spatial relationships, moving or still, between two nouns.

Of course, the adverbial use of the other prepositions is not difficult to see, especially in relation to verbs. One thinks of verbs like: "come on", "pull through" ("recover"), "go past", "come along", "stick around", and "move over". In all these cases, no following noun is suggested, and we can use all of them, except "pull through", as imperatives.

Prepositions and verbs

We considered verbs like this in some detail in Chapter 8 and, now that we are dealing with prepositions and have just finished looking at adverbs, it might be just as well to run over some of the same ground again.

Certain of the verbs we talked about in Chapter 8 are referred to as *phrasal verbs*. There is some controversy over what exactly a phrasal verb is. And we have to consider this category, because much is made of it in modern grammars.

In the sentence, "The plane will take off tomorrow", we might describe the verb part as "will take". Further thought, however, might lead us to include the word "off". And it is this part of the verb which is of interest when we are considering phrasal verbs.

Let's look at the verb "take off" in more detail. This verb consists of more than the main, or lexical verb, "take". It consists of two words, the second of which is called a particle. Two separate meanings of this two-word verb come to mind. We have the meaning applied to an aircraft when it "takes off" and we have the meaning applied to a statement like "Take off your shoes".

In the statement "Take off your shoes", the verb "take off" is transitive and means "remove"; but in the statement "The plane took off", the verb "take off" is intransitive. These are, in fact, two different phrasal verbs.

Look at this sentence:

"He took off his shoes."

Three versions of this sentence are possible:

"He took off his shoes."
"He took his shoes off."
"He took them off."

Notice that in the last two examples we have moved the particle to the end of the sentence. We have therefore split this two-word verb into two parts. In between the two parts we have inserted the object. Because we can do this, we regard this verb "take off" as a phrasal verb. But in this particular case, is the particle "off" a preposition or an adverb?

Look at this sentence:

"He took his shoes off the table."

Here, the word "off" is behaving like a normal preposition. It comes before its object: the noun phrase, "a table". And there is no way in which we could move it from that position. The preposition naturally sticks with its following noun. We could not possibly say "He took his shoes the table off."

Because the word "off" in the sentence "He took off his shoes" *can* be moved, it cannot be regarded as a preposition. It is, in fact, an adverb. A basic characteristic of a transitive phrasal verb is that its particle can be moved in this way. And the particle is always an adverbial particle, not a preposition.

The adverbial particle has a much stronger relationship with the verb than with its object. We "take off" all sorts of clothing, just as we "put on" all sorts of clothing.

In the sentence – "He took his shoes off the table" – the "off" is not so closely related to the verb. Instead, it is much more directly related to the noun phrase which follows it: "the table".

There are other similar words which could replace the word "off" here. And we could also change the verb. We could say, "Put your shoes under the table." The words "off" and "under", when used in this way are, of course, prepositions.

The fact that the word "off" can be used either as a preposition or an adverb means that we can distinguish between the transitive phrasal verb "take off" and the transitive lexical verb "take". In the sentence "Take your shoes off the table", we are using the perfectly normal, lexical verb "take". We have proved this by substituting a different lexical verb "put". And we have shown how "off" is a preposition by substituting the preposition "under".

But what about the sentence: "The plane took off"? Here we have an intransitive two-word verb, "take off". This particular verb doesn't take an object, so how do we know it's a phrasal verb?

The answer to that one is quite simple. Because the verb is intransitive, the particle following it cannot be a preposition. We can't say: "The plane took off the runway." Remember that prepositions express a relationship between a subject and an object, and that the closest of grammatical relationships exists between a preposition and its object. They have to be kept together. In the sentence "The plane

114

took off'', the possibility of such a relationship cannot occur.

There are certain verbs which are always coupled with certain prepositions. Verbs like "ask for", and "look at", for example. If we compare a two-word verb like "ask for" with our phrasal verb "take off", we can see that the two verbs do not belong to the same category.

With the phrasal verb "take off", we could make three sentences:

"He took off his clothes."
"He took his clothes off."
"He took them off."

If we try to do the same with the two-word verb "ask for" we end up with these ungrammatical sentences:

"He asked her address for."
"He asked it for."

We call two-word verbs like "ask for" and "look at" *prepositional verbs*. Remember that, with all prepositional verbs, the preposition must come before its object. If we try to move it, the sentence we are constructing becomes ungrammatical.

So, to sum up, we have established that our phrasal verb is a two-word verb, the second part of which is an adverbial particle. In our phrasal verb, the particle often appears after its object. A prepositional verb has neither of these characteristics.

But, to add to our difficulties, there are three-word verbs in English: verbs like "put up with". How are we to classify them?

Three-word verbs

The verb "put up with" has the meaning "tolerate" and is apparently indivisible. It is transitive, as in the sentence: "John could not put up with his sister for long." Since part of our definition of a phrasal verb is that it is a two-word verb, a three-word verb would be automatically excluded. In addition, our three-word verb does not appear to end with an adverbial. Neither can any of the particles appear after the object. So, how are we going to classify it?

The normal practice is to call verbs like "put up with", "look forward to", "look down on", and "cut down on" *phrasal-prepositional verbs*. This differentiates them from purely phrasal and purely prepositional verbs. They are considered to consist of a lexical verb part, followed by an adverb, followed by a preposition. These three-word verbs appear to have no special grammatical characteristics. They are all transitive and followed by an object in the normal way.

Back to prepositions
Native speakers of English know automatically which prepositions go with which verbs, and this reinforces the case for regarding prepositional verbs and their prepositions as inseparable. Foreign learners of English have to take the trouble to learn these prepositional combinations by heart, because they do not follow any obvious logical pattern. There are endless possibilities of mistakes. Why shouldn't "I will speak with him" be more natural than "I will speak to him"? There is no logical reason why this should not be so, but the fact is that the normal prepositional verb is still regarded as "speak to". These prepositional verbs have established themselves in the language over the course of centuries.

However, some might regard verbs like "speak to" as hardly prepositional verbs at all, since the meaning of the lexical verb has been retained. This is rather different from verbs like "take after", meaning "resemble", where the meaning of "take" as a separate verb is quite different. In other words, there is a strong case for regarding "speak to" as the separate lexical verb "speak" followed, in this case, by the preposition "to". We would regard the preposition in the sentence "Mary spoke to her friend" as expressing the relationship between Mary, the subject of the verb "speak", and "her friend", the object of the preposition.

A closed class
Apart from expressing the relationship between two nouns and entering into verbal combinations, prepositions also combine with other words to make a wealth of prepositional phrases.

But before we go on to look at this aspect of prepositions, it is important to recognise a special aspect of *simple prepositions* which they share with conjunctions: they are a *closed class*. This means that, unlike nouns (an *open class*), they cannot be added to. New nouns are continually being invented, but not prepositions. We have to make do with those we've been given. There is a finite number of prepositions and it's possible to draw up a complete list of them for the English language.

Prepositional complements
In sentences, although prepositions show a relationship between two nouns, there may be other elements in the sentence which come after the noun and before the preposition.

Look at this sentence:

"He pushed into the queue, angry at the delay, and the people at the front complained".

The first preposition, "into", is directly preceded by a verb, the second by an adjective, and the third by a noun. What comes after the preposition itself is known as a *prepositional complement*, and this complement in combination with the preposition itself is known as the prepositional phrase. So, the prepositional phrases here are "into the queue", "at the delay", and "at the front". Notice, by the way, that a prepositional phrase like "at the front" functions as an adverbial. In fact, prepositional phrases commonly do so.

Complex prepositions

Prepositions can be combined with other words to form *complex prepositions*. "Because of" is an example of a complex preposition formed from a conjunction and a simple preposition and "owing to" is another example, but this time formed from a participle and a simple preposition. This feature of English allows for the kind of creative increase which the closed class of simple prepositions restricts. We cannot create more simple prepositions, but the language has the potential to get around this by allowing us to create complex prepositions.

There are many three-word complex prepositions in English, which are formed by the combination of a noun preceded and followed by a simple preposition: "in order to", for example. There are four-word combinations, too, like "at the back of".

We have already considered the relation of prepositions to space and movement in space. The way in which prepositions are used to create adverbials of time is just as interesting. What would we do without phrases like "at the weekend", "for a few days", and "in ten days' time"? And think of all the adverbials we use that begin with "before", "until", "since", and "from". The way "from" combines with "to" or "until" is particularly useful: "from Monday to Wednesday", for example.

Other uses of prepositions

Another important use for prepositions is in the construction of phrases to express cause and purpose. To express the cause, or reason, for something, we can use combinations with "because of", whereas the purpose of doing something can be expressed with "in order to". But these are only the more obvious examples: there are many others.

How we do things also calls for the use of adverbials formed from prepositions. We decribe how we get to work ("by bus"), how the burglar got into the house ("by the bedroom window") and, to add one more example, how we learned more about grammar ("through reading this book").

118

It should be fairly clear now that prepositions are extremely common and powerful elements in sentence production. In spite of being part of a closed class in their simple form, they show tremendous versatility in combination with other elements of the grammar. And they have a very high profile in *idiomatic* or informal English: the kind of English we use in everyday conversation with our friends.

Phrases like "over the moon", "under the weather", "by the skin of her teeth", "for crying out loud" and "up to my eyes in it" are all examples of idiomatic phrases formed by the creative use of prepositions. These phrases, by the way, cannot be broken up. They are themselves, as a whole, expressions of particular meanings. We can't change any of the words in them, either. It is possible to buy complete books of these phrases, and foreign students of English spend a great deal of time learning them off by heart. We have to do the same with French idioms, for example.

But there are other words which combine only with particular prepositions, and this is an area which is not only notoriously difficult for all foreign students of the language but to native speakers as well. A typical example is whether we say "different from", "different than", or "different to". Another is whether we say "successful in" or "successful at". And there are many more. How do we know which is right?

The answer, of course, is to look in a very good dictionary, preferably one of the larger Oxford dictionaries. But we can't spend all our time looking these things up. What we must have is a natural confidence in our ability to speak and write our own language. Without that, we run the danger of becoming tongue-tied or over worried about how "good" we are at our own language. The answer, of course – for all of us – is "brilliant". There is no other way of describing the amazing fluency we have in a language of such complexity and variety.

So, the answer to any problems we have with prepositions is not to worry so much. The tiny amount we are *not* sure of is nothing in comparison with the huge amount we *are* sure of. And don't be worried about ending sentences with a preposition, either!

Let's just look once again at the few extra terms we have come across in this chapter:

New Grammatical Terms (11)

closed class a word class which has a finite number of items which cannot be added to

complex preposition a preposition formed from more than one word, e.g. "in order to"

open class a word class, like that of nouns, which continues to grow as more items are added

phrasal prepositional verb a three-word verb consisting of a lexical verb followed by an adverb and a preposition

phrasal verb a two-word verb which consists of a lexical verb in combination with an adverbial particle

prepositional complement the group of words added to a preposition to make an adverbial or prepositional phrase; in "for the time being", "the time being" is the prepositional complement

prepositional verb a two-word verb consisting of a lexical verb followed by a preposition

simple preposition one of the common single-word prepositions, like "in", "of", etc

Revision Eleven

1. What is the difference between an open and a closed class of words?
2. What is the difference between a simple and a complex preposition?
3. What is a prepositional complement?
4. What is the connection between prepositions and adverbial phrases?
5. What relationship do prepositions express?
6. What was our definition of a phrasal verb?
7. How is this verb different from a prepositional verb?
8. How would you explain the difference between an adverb and a preposition?
9. What have been given as the three main uses of prepositional phrases, apart from expressing spatial relationships and time?
10. Why is it not necessary to worry too much about which prepositions follow which words?

Key (Revision 11)

1.	A closed class of words is finite, but an open class of words is infinite.
2.	A simple preposition consists of one word only, but a complex preposition consists of more than one word.
3.	A prepositional complement is the group of words that follows the preposition to make up an adverbial, or prepositional phrase.
4.	Adverbial phrases often begin with prepositions.
5.	Prepositions express the relationship between two nouns, or two noun groups.
6.	Our definition of a phrasal verb was a two-word verb consisting of a lexical verb in combination with an adverb.
7.	A prepositional verb consists of a lexical verb in combination with a preposition. The preposition must come before its object.
8.	An adverb is related in some way to a previously used verb. That is its primary relationship. Unlike a preposition, it does not directly relate to a noun that follows it.
9.	Apart from time and space, prepositional phrases can express – among other things – cause, purpose, and manner.
10.	It is not necessary to worry about correctness in this area all the time: in the vast majority of cases, the native speaker will be correct anyway.

12

Joining Things Up:
Conjunctions

In a sense, the ideas of tying things up and joining them
together are much the same. We are talking about *cohesion*, which we shall be discussing in more detail in
Chapter 14. When we begin to break sentences down into
their *constituents*, we find that many constituents contain
clues which suggest a linkage to other constituents in the
sentence.

The adverbials are a good example. If we isolate an
adverbial clause – say, "because he was married" – the
word "because" tells us that a previous statement has
already been made. The same goes for clauses beginning
with similar words, like "when" for example. We can see,
immediately, that these clauses are subordinate to something else, and that they cannot stand alone. We can't say
"Because he was married" or "When I was fifteen", and
leave it at that.

Conjunctions as subordinators
For this reason, words like "because" and "when" can be
called *subordinating conjunctions* or *subordinators*. This
reminds us that they have the properties mentioned in the
previous paragraph. "When" and "because", though parts
of adverbials, have this other function for which an alternative term is required.

It cannot be emphasized too often that we must be
prepared to be reasonably flexible with our descriptive

terms. As I've said before, we can look at individual words and strings of words in different ways. This is because they can have a number of functions and enter into a number of different relationships with other words and groups of words.

This is not so different from what happens to words in non-grammatical contexts. A "woman" can be a "sister", a "daughter", a "mother", a "wife", an "aunt", a "grandmother" and so on. After we have described her gender and her maturity by the term "woman", we can also describe the other relationships into which she can enter. To do this, we change our descriptive term according to the relationship we are highlighting. In the same way nouns can function as subjects, complements, objects, and as parts of nominal groups, as well as being parts of noun phrases and clauses. We can change the descriptive term as it suits us.

Linking words

I have used the phrase "joining things up" to emphasize the linking purpose of conjunctions. Conjunctions are essentially *linking words*. But we must not oversimplify this. Linkage which remained static and undiversified would seem wooden. Not only that, it would fail to do justice to the richness and complexity of English cohesion.

Look at this, for a moment:

"... and he went to the market and he stood there looking at everything and he went to a veg stall and he stopped and he took out his money and he asked the lady for some potatoes and he put them in his bag ..."

Compare those statements with this more sophisticated version:

"After that, Mr Jakes went to the market to buy some vegetables. For a time he stood looking at the variety of choice. On one particular stall, he noticed some

125

very fine potatoes, so he decided to buy them. He approached the stall and, having taken out his purse to pay for them, asked the stall-holder for three kilograms of potatoes, which she supplied readily. Mr Jakes handed over his money and went happily on his way.''

This second paragraph has – as all blocks of language do – various cohesive devices. Apart from the very common conjunction "and", we have "after that", "so", "having" (to mean "after he had"), and "which". Try leaving these out and you will find that you are still left with a perfectly good set of sentences, but the cohesiveness is lost. We need to show the sequence of actions and how they are related.

Common conjunctions

The most common single word conjunctions are probably: "although", "and", "as", "after", "before", "because", "but", "if", "nor", "since", "that", "until", "unless", "yet".

It's fairly easy to see how "and" and "but" must be conjunctions. In the statements "James is quick-tempered and silly" and "Joan is quick-tempered but sensible", we can see immediately that omitting "and" from the first statement and "but" from the second would result in nonsense. Simply to complete the structure, some kind of word must be put between the adjectives. And, in the first sentence, to show that each adjective denotes one separate characteristic which must be added to the other we use "and". In the second sentence, we also want the two characteristics to be separate but added. However, in this case, we want to show that the second characteristic is different or contrasts in some way, so we use "but". When you think about it, this small conjunction is extraordinarily expressive.

The conjunction "yet" can be used instead of "but": "Joan is quick-tempered yet sensible". At first, the other conjunctions look rather more complicated. But try thinking of adverbials before having another look at them. Do you recall the common use of "because" to introduce a subordinate adverb clause? The conjunction "since" can often be substituted: "He didn't come to work since he was ill". So, also, can "as": "He didn't come to work as he was ill".

"Although", "after", "before", "if", "until", and "unless" are also associated with adverbial clauses, as in the following examples:

"He didn't come to work, although he was well."
"He didn't come to work after he became ill."
"He always came to work before he was ill."
"He always came to work if he was well."
"He always came to work until he became ill."
"He always came to work unless he was ill."

In each of these sentences, the removal of the conjunction or "joining word" kills the relationship between the two clauses. "He always came to work" and "He was well", for instance, remain completely separate statements.

"Nor" and "that"

In our short list of conjunctions, we are left with "nor" and "that". These two conjunctions do not appear to be as simple to explain as those we have just considered. But a little thought will bring to mind the connection between "nor" and "and". The former is, in fact, a negative form of the latter. We can show this by comparing the sentence "James didn't come to work and he wasn't ill" with "James didn't come to work nor was he ill" or, perhaps better, "James neither came to work nor was he ill". The conjunction "nor" allows us to relate and join the two clauses using a different verb structure. Again, the removal of the conjunction destroys the linkage and the relationship between the two clauses.

In the sentence "James told me that he was coming back to work", the word "that" is regarded as a conjunction because it joins the subordinate clause "he was coming back to work" to the main clause "James told me". Again, take out the conjunction and you have two unrelated, separate statements.

Co-ordinating conjunctions

Where the conjunction joins two equal nouns, clauses, or phrases, we call it a *co-ordinating conjunction*. In the sentences we have been considering, the conjunctions like "because", "although", "after", and so on, were all subordinating conjunctions for the reasons I've given above. But in our earlier sentence saying that "James is quick tempered and silly", we describe the conjunction as co-ordinating.

The way co-ordinating conjunctions operate between phrases and clauses is easily demonstrated by the examples: "James is quick to lose his temper and invariably rather stupid" and "James lost his temper and struck the policeman". Both phrases and clauses have equal status in their particular sentences.

If we regard the one word conjunctions we have mentioned as *simple conjunctions*, we can speak of conjunctions which consist of two or more words as *complex conjunctions*. I am thinking of such conjunctions as "so that", "as if", and "as soon as". It will be seen that these complex conjunctions function exactly like simple conjunctions, as the following sentences show:

"James was really ill so that he couldn't get on with his work."
"He went completely white as if he were in pain."
"He went straight to bed as soon as he got home."

Connectors

There are certain words which appear to be synonyms for our conjunctions, but which behave in a rather different way. Whereas there appears to be no significant difference between "but" and "yet", "however" and "nevertheless" and "on the other hand" appear to be in a rather different category.

Compare these sentences, for example:

"James is quick-tempered and silly but Joan is quick tempered but sensible."
"James is quick-tempered and silly yet Joan is quick-tempered but sensible."
"James is quick-tempered and silly. However, Joan is quick-tempered and sensible."
"James is quick-tempered and silly. Nevertheless, Joan is quick-tempered and sensible." '
"James is quick-tempered and silly. On the other hand, Joan is quick-tempered and sensible."

What will be noticed immediately is that we have to put full-stops before these words. This suggests that the way they link groups of words is rather different from that of conjunctions. They *are* linking words, but they seem to link sentences that would otherwise be separate, rather than linking units within the same sentence. For this reason, we prefer to call them *sentence connectors* or, to use a more technical term, *conjuncts*. We shall have more to say about this kind of thing in a later chapter.

For the time being, it is interesting to note the flexibility of placing which connectors demonstrate in comparison with the relative inflexibility of conjunctions. In the sentence "However, Joan is quick-tempered and sensible", the conjunct "however" can be placed after "Joan", after "is", after "quick-tempered" and after "sensible". But there is no way we can interrupt the linking of "and" and "sensible". Even if we use "but" to begin a sentence – or, in other words, to imitate a conjunct – it will not adapt to the flexibility of "however". If we replace "however" and make our sentence "But Joan is quick-tempered and sensible", there is no way we can move the word "but". We have here a real difference between a conjunction and a conjunct.

"Pseudo" conjunctions
Now look at the sentences below:

"I'll give her a ring directly I get home."
"I'll give her a ring the instant I get home."
"I'll give her a ring, seeing you are here."

In all of these sentences, we see words which look unlike conjunctions but which are functioning in the same way. The word "directly" looks like an adverb, the word "instant" looks like a noun, and the word "seeing" looks like a verb. In some grammar descriptions you will see words like these three described respectively as *adverbial conjunctions*, *nominal conjunctions*, and *verbal conjunctions*. Though initially confusing, these terms do demonstrate the way certain words have a flexibility of function beyond their word class. But it is their function rather than their origin that really determines what they are.

As I've said, we shall be considering linkage in more detail when we look at English cohesion at above sentence level. For the time being, here are the new terms you have been introduced to in this chapter:

New Grammatical Terms (12)

adverbial conjunction a conjunction which looks like an adverb

cohesion the way a text is bound together into a whole

complex conjunction a conjunction which consists of more than one word

conjunct another word for 'sentence connector'

constituents the parts of a sentence

co-ordinating conjunction a conjunction which links two equal units

linking word a word which links other words, phrases, or clauses together

nominal conjunction a conjunction which looks like a noun

sentence connector a word which looks like a conjunction but which links two sentences

simple conjunction a conjunction which consists of one word only

subordinating conjunction a conjunction which introduces a subordinate clause

subordinator as above

verbal conjunction a conjunction which looks like a verb

Revision Twelve

1. What is cohesion?
2. What are constituents?
3. What is another name for the term 'subordinating conjunction'?
4. What is another simple name for 'conjunction'?
5. What is the difference between a simple and a complex conjunction?
6. What do we call a conjunction which links two equal units?
7. What is the name for a word which looks like a conjunction but links sentences?
8. What is another name for the above?
9. What term could you use for a conjunction which looked like an adverb?
10. In the sentence "I'll give you a ring, seeing you are here", what kind of word is "seeing"?

Key (Revision 12)

1. The way a text is bound together to make a whole.
2. The units which make up the sentence.
3. 'Subordinator'.
4. 'Linking word'.
5. A simple conjunction consists of only one word whereas a complex conjunction consists of more than one word.
6. A 'co-ordinating conjunction'.
7. A 'sentence connector'*.
8. A 'conjunct'*.
   (* these last two are interchangeable)
9. An 'adverbial conjunction'.
10. A 'verbal conjunction'.

13

What Goes with What?
Punctuation Does Matter

As I write this, I have to bear in mind, all the time, where I want to keep the various parts of my sentence together and where I want to keep other parts separate. Languages have their own ways of doing this, and writers in a particular language have to follow the conventions of that particular language. There can be no anarchists where languages are concerned.

Because all languages are rule governed, none of us can do just as we like with them. People who are exceptionally gifted in writing a language, such as poets, can, and do, take what appear to be liberties. But they know what they are doing. At least, we hope they do.

We lesser mortals have to be quite sure about what the conventions in our language are. We must be aware, for example, that our written sentences are expected to begin with a capital letter. We also have to be aware that our sentences are expected to end with a full-stop. And a full-stop is a punctuation mark.

It's not difficult to imagine a page of written English which contains no full-stops. If you've ever seen, or received, a page of English without full-stops, you will, no doubt, have spent an irritating, or fascinating, time deciphering it. It all depends on your personality, or state of mind at the time.

Punctuation, however, is not about what type of people

134

we are: it's about what message we intend to convey. If we want to communicate chaos, then unpunctuated nonsense will do very well. But if we are concerned – as we should be – about communicating effectively, then we need to know what punctuation marks are available to us and what conventions there are about their use.

This is not to say that everyone uses all the punctuation marks equally often, and that there are no differences whatsoever in their use. Of course not. Because languages, like most things in this life, are subject to gradual change, so the conventions of punctuation also change over time. Just as there are obvious differences between what our grandparents thought right and proper and the way we behave today, so there are differences in how they punctuated their sentences and how we punctuate ours.

What we have to do is become familiar with the various punctuation marks available to us and how they are used nowadays. But before we go into this in more detail, we have to give the matter a bit of thought.

We have already agreed, I hope, that we need full-stops at the end of our sentences. If we don't put them there in our writing, our readers will have a lot of trouble deciding where one sentence ends and the next begins. Because we are polite, kind, considerate people, we don't want to cause our readers unnecessary and irritating trouble. We want to help them to understand what we have written.

Each sentence that we write is made up of parts. Not only individual words, but groups of words as well. The first sentence in this paragraph has no punctuation marks in it. There is simply a full-stop at the end to show where it finishes. It doesn't appear to need any more punctuation. If you take the commas out of some of the other sentences in this chapter, however, you might find the sentences a little difficult to follow.

Look at the word "however" in the last sentence of the previous paragraph. If the word "however" began with a capital and there was no comma after it, it would become quite a different kind of "however". However you looked at it, something would have changed.

Punctuation makes a difference

It is because punctuation marks can make such a big difference to what we are trying to say that we have to be most careful about how we use them. Whereas, in that sentence, I can get away with no commas at all, I have, in this sentence – specially constructed for the purpose – to be quite sure, within the conventions of usage, that I am using commas where necessary. Of course, what we write can usually be written more simply and with fewer commas, but we shall be considering that in more detail later. For the time being, we are training ourselves to be more 'punctuation sensitive'.

A complex sentence with a comma after every word would be just as confusing as a complex sentence with no commas at all. We have to know which parts of the sentence are to be taken together. There are, as we know, words in a sentence which belong to a particular group. We cannot separate these words from their grammatical group without doing serious damage to the sentence as a whole.

In a sentence like ''The huge gorilla strolled into the crowded supermarket and stole three enormous bunches of ripe bananas'' we can't put a comma after 'huge' because it would separate two words which grammatically belong together. Our punctuation, remember, is intended to make things clearer, not the reverse. Good punctuation never conflicts with the rules of grammar: it works *with* the grammar to improve communication.

Small children can be taught, fairly early, when and how to use full-stops, but it takes rather longer to learn how to use commas. The reasons for this should now be fairly obvious. What is not normally obvious, however, is how complicated and difficult the effective use of commas really is. We could be quite unaware of all the other punctuation marks and still be able to communicate reasonably well, but commas – like full-stops – are so intimately bound up with the grammar that they pose by far the greatest difficulties.

Because this is so, let's concentrate on the other punctuation marks first, and then come back to commas later.

You should find the other punctuation marks relatively simple.

The exclamation mark

The easiest punctuation mark to use is the *exclamation mark*. We can use it when we want to show anger, excitement, or surprise: "You should have seen his face!" Because we don't normally express our emotions in formal writing, it is uncommon to find exclamation marks in letters from bank managers and solicitors, for example. And we would never find them in legal contracts. Their use is a flexible and personal matter. We can even use two exclamation marks together, although such usage is usually restricted to notes and letters between intimate friends.

Dashes and brackets

Dashes or *brackets* are interchangeable, really. They are used for the equivalent of asides, or bits of extra information. You should always be able to take out the information within the dashes – or brackets – without altering the sense of the sentence. If you took out the words "or brackets" from the previous sentence, it would still make sense. Brackets can be used (it's a matter of personal preference really) instead of dashes, but it's better to stick to one or the other within a particular piece of writing.

Colons

Colons can be very useful. You must have noticed their use before lists of various kinds, and this is their most common use. Often, they come after phrases such as "the following" or "as follows". "The list of ingredients is as follows: cheese, eggs, flour ...". You will also have seen colons used in written conversations or before quotations. Whatever you do, never use a colon followed by a dash: the dash is quite unnecessary and totally unconventional. And when you want to add an explanation – as in the previous sentence – a colon is a very useful punctuation mark.

Quotation marks

The use for *quotation marks* is pretty obvious. Whenever you include a quotation from a book or from what somebody said, you should always put quotation marks round it. You have two choices: single or double. Which to use depends really on personal preference. Normally, doubles are the most common, but single quotation marks are useful in the same way that round and square brackets are in mathematics. When you have a quotation within a quotation, it becomes absolutely necessary to use both: "Churchill said 'We will fight on the beaches' but he wasn't talking about football hooligans".

Apostrophes

The *apostrophe* is necessary when we want to show that Arthur's book really belongs to Arthur. In other words, it shows possession. If we want to show plural possession, instead of putting the high comma before the "s" we put it after. "The prisoners' breakfasts" refers to the breakfasts of several prisoners, not just one. The apostrophe is also used to show that something has been left out. When you write "isn't" instead of "is not", the apostrophe is placed where the letter is missing. But be careful with "its". Because two forms are possible – the contraction for "it is" and the possessive – the convention is not to use the apostrophe with the possessive. We say, "It's a nice day". But we also say, "The dog has lost its basket".

These few comments about the use of various punctuation marks are all you need for the time being. Once you get the idea, there are plenty of books around which give practice exercises in this kind of thing. But we are primarily interested in why we have punctuation marks in the first place, and what such things have to do with grammar. Which brings us back to the comma.

Commas

A sentence like "All the students who were sick left the room" is what we call *ambiguous*. In other words, it has two possible meanings. It could mean that all the students were sick and they left the room, or it could mean that only those students who were sick left the room.

It is customary – or the convention – in written English to use commas to show the meaning we intend. This is especially interesting because it lays bare the whole business of showing what goes with what. If you look at the sentence carefully, you should be able by now to separate it into its constituent parts. The part beginning with the relative pronoun "who" stands out. We know it begins a relative clause and that the relative clause ends with the adjective "sick": "who are sick". We could take out the relative clause and be left with the main clause: "All the students left the room". The main clause, of course, could stand as a sentence in its own right.

If we want to say that all the students left the room, it is customary in writing to put commas before and after the relative, or adjective, clause: "All the students, who were sick, left the room". This shows that this subordinate clause – "who were sick" – contains additional information about the subject – "the students" – and this additional information could be left out.

But what about if we want to say that only the students who were sick left the room? If this is what we really want to say, the convention is to leave out the commas and regard "the students who were sick" as the subject. This subject cannot be broken up in any way. We can no longer take out the words "who were sick", because these words are part of the subject. We therefore write the sentence without commas: "All the students who were sick left the room".

If you can follow this – and it shouldn't be too difficult – you are probably beginning to see the importance of commas. It is quite impossible to remove the ambiguity in the sentence illustrated without using or not using that particular punctuation mark. But we have to follow the convention. There is only one way of showing the difference and we have to keep to it.

This is particularly important. We can't expect to break conventions. There is a conventional way of doing things in punctuation just as there is in grammar. In the same way

139

that the grammar of a language is a commonly understood way of doing things, so too is punctuation. We can't mix words up in any order, nor can we randomly put commas everywhere.

It used to be thought that one put commas in so called 'breathing spaces'. But this is to confuse the issue. When we read something aloud, the pauses do tend to correspond with written commas and full-stops. But this is because we are reading, and responding to, the punctuation that is already there. The punctuation is helping us to read. And this is the whole point: the writer has used punctuation to help us interpret what he or she has written.

It is important to be very sparing with commas until you know exactly what you are doing. One way to become sensitive to their use is to read the best modern writers very carefully, noticing how and when they use commas. Leading articles in the quality newspapers are a good guide, too. As you become more confident, your own use of commas will be part of your own style: without breaking the conventions, you will be increasingly able to tie in your punctuation with your own personal use of the language.

There are a few obvious and stable uses for the comma. Adverbial clauses – for instance, those beginning with "if", "when", "although", and so on – when they come first in a sentence, are always followed by a comma: "If she rings, tell her I'll be at her place at six". Single adverbs, when they come between parts of the verb or between the subject and the verb are always preceded and followed by commas: "Richard, however, decided not to come after all". Once you get used to noticing the commas around very common words and phrases – such as "however", "certainly", "of course" – then you will soon get used to doing the same thing yourself. And, of course, you always need commas to separate words in a list, whether nouns or adjectives.

Semi-colons
Another punctuation mark – the *semi-colon* – is relevant here. There are times when our list of items, each one

separated by a comma, needs dividing into separate groups. It is here where the semi-colon comes in particularly useful. In a list – "cheese, eggs, apples; shoes, socks, shirts; paraffin, petrol, oil" – it is, as I have shown here, convenient to be able to use the semi-colon to separate food, clothing, and fuel.

Semi-colons are also used to show the connection between two statements. On certain occasions, you might feel that a full-stop completely separates two statements that you would prefer to keep together.

Look at these sentences:

"So I caught the bus instead. It stops just outside my house."

You might feel that the second of these two sentences is so closely connected to the first, that you want to show this close connection. Unfortunately, you can't use a comma because it isn't regarded as strong enough. It is customary, in English, to use the semi-colon for this purpose: "So I caught the bus; it stops just outside my house". If you decide to do this, remember to remove the capital letter.

Don't be overwhelmed

Once again, it is very important not to let yourself be overwhelmed by the problems connected with punctuation. There are always problems – even for good writers – in trying to put meanings across. Each writer does what is possible within the constraints which language imposes. This is why the very best writers in a language strain the language to its utmost without actually breaking the grammar. They are trying to express the deepest and most complex meanings that the language will bear.

We are all of us engaged, at various levels, in the same process. It is important that we don't lose sight of that fact. The study of grammar is not something reserved for a few unusually gifted persons but is beneficial to all of us in some degree. Whenever we speak and write, we are using the grammar of our own language. We are simply studying something we already know and use, but not perhaps as consciously as we might.

Punctuation has to be regarded in much the same light. None of us can avoid using punctuation when we write our language. It will do us no harm to consider what exactly we are doing and why we are doing it.

And here, once again, are the new terms you have been introduced to in this chapter:

New Grammatical Terms (13)

ambiguity when a sentence has two possible meanings

apostrophe written like this ' and used to show possession or when a letter has been missed out

brackets written like this ( ) can be used instead of dashes

colon written like this : and used before a list, before an explanation, or before someone speaks

dashes written like this – and used before and after a word or phrase which is additional or extra, like an aside, and could be excluded

exclamation mark written like this ! and used in informal English to show surprise, delight, or anger

quotation marks written like this " " or ' ' and used before and after quotations or before and after someone speaks. They are sometimes called "speech marks". Doubles or singles can be used, and the use of both is especially useful when we quote someone's quotation from someone else

semi-colon written like this ; and used to separate items divided by commas into groups. Also used to divide two statements where the use of a full-stop would be too strong, and a comma too weak.

Revision Thirteen

Here are a few questions to check that you absorbed the information in this chapter.
1.   Can you identify these four punctuation marks? : ! ' ;
2.   Can you explain, in order, how each one is used?
3.   See if you can punctuate this paragraph. The layout also needs to be clearer:

Mr Smith was unhappy He had as usual had a boring day He said to his wife Mary Ive had a boring day and its all your fault But Mary she always felt like this couldnt be bothered to answer him Mary he shouted Answer me But Mary remained silent This shouted Mr Smith is as Churchill said a situation up with which I will not put

Key (Revision 13)

1. (i) colon (ii) exclamation mark (iii) apostrophe (iv) semi-colon
2. (i) before a list, before an explanation, or before someone speaks (ii) to show surprise, delight, or anger (iii) to show possession or when a letter has been missed out (iv) to separate items divided by commas into groups, and to separate two statements where a full-stop or comma would not be suitable
3. Mr Smith was unhappy. He had, as usual, had a boring day. He said to his wife, Mary: "I've had a boring day and it's all your fault". But Mary – she always felt like this – couldn't be bothered to answer him.

   "Mary!" he shouted. "Answer me!"

   But Mary remained silent.

   "This," shouted Mr Smith, "is, as Churchill said, 'a situation up with which I will not put'!"

NOTE

There are other correct ways of punctuating this.

You could write: "Mary, I've had a boring day and it's all your fault."

You could write: "Mary," he shouted, "answer me!"

And you could miss out the exclamation mark at the end and replace with a full-stop.

14

The Shape of the Whole

The time has come to stop thinking of details all the time and, instead, to try and imagine everything on a broader canvas. At some stage, it is necessary to stop looking at everything with a microscope, or magnifying glass, and look out of the window. We move from interior design to landscapes.

This isn't easy. For years, parents, teachers, bosses and busy-bodies have forced us to concentrate on spelling, punctuation, and correctness at the expense of everything else. In this book, too, there has been a lot of emphasis on sentence-level grammar. And, of course, we have to begin somewhere. But it would be a serious mistake to lose touch with wider issues. Each small part of our grammar, from each individual phoneme or letter, belongs to a wider, deeper, and larger world.

I don't know if you are a bookish person or not but, if you are, you will probably be surrounded by books. Your shelves will be crammed with them and sagging under the weight. And what a weight! Take any of those books down, or simply pick up the book you are currently reading, and you will have in your hand something which is a completed entity. From the binding to the last page, the book you are holding has been given substance and shape.

Style
What we have to imagine is a great tide of language,

sweeping through the centuries. We have no knowledge of its beginning and we have no intimation of its ending. Through the course of its history, that language has been moulded and changed by the people who spoke it and, later, wrote it. But each speaker gave that language something of himself. Each speaker spoke it and wrote it in an individual way. That individual way of using the language had to be understood by everyone else at the time, but nevertheless it was, in subtle ways, slightly different from everyone else's usage. We call that individual style an *idiolect*.

The book you picked up or took down from your shelves is marked by someone's idiolect. Sometimes, that idiolect is strong enough for us to talk of a particular *style* of writing. Indeed, there is a separate part of *linguistics* which concentrates on this aspect of language: called *stylistics*.

Perhaps you have already read all or part of the book you looked at. I wonder what you remember of it? Do you remember the *plot* or *narrative*, the characters or *characterisation*, or the style? Of course, the book may not be a story, or work of *fiction*. It could be a book about something factual, in which case we would call it a work of *non-fiction*. But even works of non-fiction can have their own stylistic interest. Charles Darwin's "The Origin of Species" is read as much for its style as its content, and the same goes for Gibbon's "The Decline and Fall of the Roman Empire". And there are very many books in this category.

Judging literature

The process of evaluating books and deciding which book is superior to others is part of what is called *literary criticism*. Any book on your shelves, or in any bookshop or library, can be evaluated in some way. Literary criticism, naturally, restricts itself to what is considered to be 'literature', although the definition of what is true literature has always been a matter of dispute. There is unanimity over what one might call the 'great' writers – Shakespeare, for instance – but lesser talents are always argued about. In the case of modern writers, this is very much the case. It is very difficult for most people to understand how one can properly criticise works of literature, and the invention of modern critical theories has made the whole subject even more difficult. Judging literature is like judging people: opinions differ so much as to what is 'good'.

Stylistics, however, is not concerned with what is good or bad but, instead, with the linguistic characteristics of what is called *text*. To the linguist, any piece of writing, or text, is interesting for its own sake, whether it be regarded as literature or not. The better the linguist is able to describe the nature of a particular text, the better able literary critics should be to talk about what is actually there. But, unfortunately, this is not the case. Literary critics tend to talk about narrative and characterisation, and so on, but they rarely talk about text in any meaningful way. And the reason for this is probably because they don't know how. The expert in stylistics, on the other hand, knows how to describe an author's style but is not concerned to evaluate it against any kind of 'literary' measure.

Any book we might like to consider can be analysed from the point of view of stylistics. And we would expect a book of instruction to have rather a different style from a thriller. This is surely something which most of us would regard as obvious. But how obvious?

Such a question brings us up against the problem of exactly how text is to be described. Strangely enough, at sentence level you already know how to do this. You should by now be able to take any sentence and break it up into its constituent parts. If you listed what you found in one sentence and then did the same under similar headings for other sentences in the same book, you would be making a detailed analysis of the writer's style. This is what stylistics, basically, is.

This might, at first thought, appear intimidating. After all, although you have read this book so far very carefully, there are still parts of it which you aren't too sure of. In fact, you still find yourself looking back to the notes at the end of earlier chapters to determine what a particular grammatical term means.

All this is, of course, quite normal and natural. None of us can absorb a load of technical detail at one sitting. We have to go back constantly and revise what we thought we'd understood and learned. But, having allowed for that, can we really describe what is there with confidence? Yes, we can. Let's try it with this paragraph.

Analysing the sentence again

In the first sentence we have a subject "All this", which consists of a demonstrative "this" with a premodifier "all". The subject is followed by the verb "be" in the present simple. We then have an adverbial of manner, separated by two commas, which modifies the whole sentence. This adverbial is followed by a subject complement which consists of two adjectives, "normal" and "natural", separated by a conjunction. Our sentence consists of a single clause: there are no subsidiary clauses.

Our second sentence, beginning with "none", has the subject, "none of us". This subject is a noun phrase consisting of two pronouns separated by a preposition. The subject of our sentence is followed by a main verb "absorb" premodified by an auxiliary "can". This verb phrase is followed by the object of the main verb: "a load of technical detail", which is a complex noun phrase consisting of the noun "detail" premodified by the adjective "technical" and further modified by the noun phrase "a load of". This object is followed by the prepositional phrase, or adjunct, used as an adverbial: "at one sitting".

We could continue this rather tedious process by analysing further sentences in this manner and, by doing so, we would build up a stylistic picture of the writer's prose style. We might discover that the writer used complex sentences with lots of subordinate clauses rather than simple sentences, that he tended to use a lot of modification, that he made excessive use of commas, that he rarely used the present simple tense, and so on. And, although tedious, the exercise would reveal more about the writer's style than we could gather from a casual sampling. But, even if we went through a whole book doing this, using a computer to help us collect all the data, we would, in the end, be unable to see the wood for the trees.

There is a higher level

In order to see the wood, or the book as a whole, we have to move from sentence level analysis to analysis at a higher level. The book has length, or quantity, and this total length, although certainly divided up into sentences at one level, is further divided up into larger quantitative measures. There are paragraphs and chapters, for instance.

The question naturally arises as to how all these sentences which go to make paragraphs, and all these paragraphs which go to make chapters, are connected. And, come to that, how are the chapters connected to make one whole book?

Textual cohesion

What we are considering here is *textual cohesion*: what makes our text as a whole hang together. *Linguisticians*, to use a term which is descriptive but not particularly favoured, regard spoken English as also constituting 'text'. When such spoken English is set out on the page in *phonetic transcription*, the idea begins to make sense. And because all text presupposes communication, even if only with oneself, the common term for text considered in this way is *discourse*. Hence, analysis of this discourse is referred to as *discourse analysis*.

If we are considering any kind of text, including a complete book, we are considering something which is externally related to readers and listeners. It is also, of course, internally related to itself and its creator. So we have to imagine a complex network of relationships. This shouldn't be too difficult if we keep in mind the kind of relationships we considered at sentence level. Think of relative pronouns, for example.

When I begin a sentence with the word "however", it becomes immediately obvious that I am referring to something that has gone before. The word also signals a qualification of some kind: we are not to take what has gone before as entirely satisfactory. Because adverbials like this can be slotted into different parts of the sentence and don't seem to alter the essential grammar of the sentence in any way, they are sometimes called *sentence adverbials*. I mention this because such sentence adverbials can help us with the notion of *connectives*: those units which help give cohesion to our text.

If we compare sentences like: "Jill was, however, ill in bed", "Jill was ill in bed, however", and "However, Jill was ill in bed", it is impossible not to feel strongly – in each case – that we need to know more about what came before this statement. Sentence adverbials like this are extremely important in this respect.

Anaphoric devices

We have already noticed how important pronouns are, and how pedantic and dull sentences would be if we repeated the noun all the time instead. But pronouns are also important above the sentence level.

Look at these sentences, for a moment:

"When Mary got home, she was feeling totally exhausted. She opened the door and immediately noticed a card lying on the doormat. She picked the card up and read it carefully. It was from her brother in India."

It will become immediately apparent that there are a number of pronouns in this short paragraph. The interesting thing about these pronouns, however, is that they can refer to nouns outside the sentences in which they occur as well as within them. In the first sentence, "she" refers back to Mary in the same sentence. In the second sentence, "she" refers back to the proper noun "Mary" in the first sentence. There is a further "she" in the next sentence, and the possessive pronoun "her" in the last sentence also refers back to "Mary".

In linguistics, we call such back reference *anaphora*, and

a unit which is used for back reference is called an *anaphoric device*. It will be quite obvious now that pronouns must be very common anaphoric devices.

A text which simply relied on anaphoric devices to make connections and give cohesion would be curiously deficient, however. We need also to look forward. As the text is being created, it is moving on, looking towards what will come next. If you think about it, it would be impossible to speak a sentence without somehow imagining it in your mind first.

Think of someone giving a lecture. The lecturer not only checks to see everyone has understood by saying something like "All right?" or "Okay?", but also says things like "Right" or "Now" or "Next" to show that he or she is moving on to the next stage. Meanwhile, the lecturer is continuously monitoring what has gone before and what is to come.

Cataphoric devices

What about a sentence like "If she had the money, Mary could go and see her brother in India"? Here, the pronoun "she" is not referring back to Mary but forward to her. In this case, we refer to the process as *cataphora* and the units in question as *cataphoric devices*. Such cataphoric devices anticipate what is to come rather than refer back to what has gone before. Again, it isn't difficult to imagine such a device being applied higher than the sentence level, as in the following:

> "It was purposeful, and even slightly sinister. It was intent on the hunt and nothing else. There was a meanness, a hunger, about its every movement. But throughout the course of its journey towards its prey, the tiger made no sound."

Here the pronouns anticipate the noun which will follow, and are typical examples of cataphora.

We have to imagine, then, not only the mental monitoring which goes on when someone is creating language, but

152

the linguistic devices which show that this is going on and which hold the text together.

Sometimes, these linguistic devices are quite subtle, as when the final chapter of a book ends with the words "and that is what all this has been about". Here, the two anaphoric devices "that" and "this" refer, in a complex way, to everything that has gone before. The word "this" could also have cataphoric reference if, for example, the subject is considered as continuing in some way into the future.

On many occasions, back-reference is relatively clear and simple, as when an author begins a chapter with the words, "In my previous chapter . . ." There is, in fact, a whole range of devices, from the very simple and obvious to the most complex, which give a text cohesion.

As we have noticed before, it isn't easy to define exactly what a sentence is. Certainly not before it has been created, anyway. Once the sentence is there on paper, it is comparatively simple to describe what is actually there. This is the case with paragraphs, too.

So what is a paragraph, really?

Just as most of us are familiar with the fairly useless definition of a sentence ("a complete thought in words") so most of us are also familiar with fairly useless definitions of a paragraph ("the introduction of a new idea", and so on). But how exactly *do* we define a paragraph?

I don't myself really think it's necessary to try and define a paragraph. It's far better to imagine a long chunk of writing which is undivided by punctuation of any kind and start from there. Let's do that.

". . . and that is exactly what I thought how do you get a subject like this in true perspective is there a proper method or do we leave it all to chance if you read books on it there are so many points of view that things become even more confusing than they were before probably the best way is to take things step by step in that way the subject becomes more

manageable or more digestible if you like we read
carefully selected parts of various books make notes
and gradually come to a considered conclusion . . .''

Forget about the punctuation for the ·time being, and
concentrate on the words. I think most of us will notice the
first question beginning with ''how'' and, later, the word
''probably''. It seems as if there are definite stops there
which are stronger than the normal beginnings of sentences. If, having noticed these words, we arranged the
material into three paragraphs, we would come up with
this:

''. . . and that is exactly what I thought.

How do you get a subject like this in true perspective? Is there a proper method? Or do we leave it all to
chance? If you read books on it, there are so many
points of view that things become even more confusing than they were before.

Probably the best way is to take things step by step.
In that way, the subject becomes more manageable or
more digestible, if you like: we read carefully selected
parts of various books, make notes, and gradually
come to a considered conclusion.''

Now this isn't the only way to arrange this segment of
language. If you compare the front pages of popular
tabloids with those of the broadsheet quality newspapers,
you will immediately notice different ways of paragraphing. Which is the best?

Well, as a general rule, it probably pays to be reasonably
conservative in these matters. If you wanted a model
pronunciation – one that was universally acceptable – the
pronunciation of a TV newsreader would be a good bet.
Similarly, an English person would be safer to imitate
''The Times'' rather than ''The Sun''.

If you cast your mind back, you will remember what we
said earlier in the book about custom and convention.
Paragraphing is very much a matter of convention or
custom. In fact, much of written presentation is just this.

That's why there are such things as "house styles". Look through the reference section of your library or bookshop and, sooner or later, you will come across a guide to presentation issued under the umbrella of a particular magazine or newspaper. And if you yourself do any free-lance writing, you will probably have received a sheet from your editor telling you how the magazine prefers its copy to be presented.

There is more than one way
So, the unfortunate truth – or fortunate, depending on how you see it – is that there is no one way of paragraphing, any more than there is one way of beginning or ending chapters of a book. There are conventions, as I've said, but they are plural rather than singular. In language, imitation matters. If you spend all your time reading popular maga-zines and reading popular newspapers, as well as reading advertisements, you will tend to imitate what you read. The only cure for what you, or others, don't like about the way you write is to choose different models. And that goes for all of us.

What is 'literature'?
One final matter needs to be cleared up: the difference between language and literature. This is relevant here, because literature tends to be thought of as a whole, and its texts are whole texts rather than sentences. These texts may vary from short poems, through plays, to long novels. Why are they literature? And why do we regard English Language and English Literature as being different?

It's true that in examinations, for example, there are separate examinations in both, and school timetables some-times give them different allocations. But, although all literature is obviously expressed through language, there are conflicting ideas about what literature really is. Indeed, there are famous definitions scattered throughout the "Oxford Dictionary of Quotations" and elsewhere, but all are debatable.

This is because the definition of literature involves value judgements. All so-called "good" writing does. But the criteria for such judgements are variable enough to cause continuous debate. This is why the list of set books in literature examinations varies from generation to generation.

The judgement of what is "literature" is supposedly decided by literary critics, and literary criticism is still a subject read about and lectured on at universities. It is regarded as a valid academic discipline. But where linguistics, for example, fits into all this remains debatable. The evolution of stylistics has begun to break down subject barriers, but much remains to be done in this area.

The truth is that no-one can talk about so-called "literature" without considering the language in which it is communicated. What makes one writer superior to another must have something to do with the way that he or she uses language. If it doesn't, then to talk about "writing" at all becomes meaningless. We cannot regard language as a static, permanently unchanging vehicle for the expression of thoughts and ideas and feelings. The thoughts, feelings, and ideas are inextricably embedded in the language through which they are expressed. And, as we have said before, the expression will vary from person to person.

Perhaps, the reason why there is still an unnatural separation between literature and language is because it is relatively easy to pronounce on ideas, thoughts, and feelings. We do it all the time: at home, on trains, in pubs, or wherever. But to talk meaningfully about language means taking the trouble to learn something about its grammar and the descriptive terms which are necessary to communicate that knowledge. This is something which, hopefully, we are all finding easier at this late stage in our journey through this book. And there is no doubt whatsoever that such knowledge will make it easier to consider so-called "literature" in a more comprehensive and meaningful way.

Finally, here is the list of new terms we have met in this chapter:

New Grammatical Terms (14)

anaphora back-reference in texts

anaphoric device any unit which effects back-reference

cataphora forward-reference in texts

cataphoric device any unit which effects forward-reference

characterisation the way the characters in a story are made real

discourse linguistic communication

discourse analysis the analysis of spoken and written text

fiction something imagined

idiolect the person's individual way of using language

linguistician an expert in linguistics

linguistics the study of language in all its aspects

literary criticism making value judgements about literature

narrative story

non-fiction something factual or true

phonetic transcription sounds translated into phonetic symbols

plot the way the story develops

sentence adverbial an adverbial which is outside the different parts of sentence structure

stylistics the study of language use, especially in writing

textual cohesion the way a piece of writing holds together

Revision Fourteen

1. What would you call the personal way somebody speaks and writes?
2. What wider subject is grammar part of?
3. What is 'stylistics'?
4. What two basic elements does a narrative contain?
5. What is the difference between fiction and non-fiction?
6. What do we call the academic judgement of literature?
7. What is 'textual cohesion'?
8. What system would you use to record the way somebody spoke?
9. What is the difference between cataphora and anaphora?
10. What is 'discourse analysis'?

Key (Revision 14)

1. That person's 'idiolect'.
2. Grammar is part of 'linguistics'.
3. Stylistics is the study of the similarities, differences, and particular nature of texts.
4. A narrative contains plot and characterisation.
5. 'Fiction' is imagined, whereas 'non-fiction' refers to facts and material which is not imagined or made up.
6. We call that 'literary criticism'.
7. This is the way a text hangs together as a whole.
8. 'Phonetic transcription'.
9. 'Cataphora' refers to forward reference in texts, and 'anaphora' refers to backward reference.
10. 'Discourse analysis' is the study of the way in which communication takes place via written and spoken language.

15

Back to Basics

By now, you're probably feeling the burden of all this weight of terminology. So, to rebuild your confidence and demonstrate that you really have absorbed more than you think you have, this chapter will be devoted to revision.

However, before we get down to basics, I hope you've studied the list of definitions at the end of each chapter, done the revision exercises and checked your answers. After that, you should have gone back and reread any problem sections.

If you haven't done these things, then you will obviously have a little difficulty with this chapter. You can choose to go ahead with it, in spite of misgivings, or you can have a read through the definitions at the end of each previous chapter before you start. It's up to you. I don't want to make you feel that this book has, after all, turned into a typical text-book like all the others. It should still be learner-friendly, to coin a phrase.

Anyway, what I'm going to do is to give you clear outlines of what has gone before, but I'm going to leave gaps which you can fill with the appropriate terms. Each short incomplete outline is followed by a completed outline. Always make sure the completed outline is covered before you begin to fill in the gaps.

After you've worked through the outline and filled as many of the gaps as you can, you can either move on to the completed outline which follows, or refer back to earlier parts of the book. The completed outline is there for you when you're ready to use it. So, here goes:

OUTLINE ONE

The complete system of a language is called its - - - - . This system uses words and arranges them in order, and this order is called - - - - . The various patterns which these words form are combined to make sentences, and the words in these sentences can be allocated to various parts of speech or - - - - - - - - .

The word, or group of words, which begins the sentence is called the - - - - of the sentence. The - - - - of a sentence, in English, is normally followed by a - - - - - . If the - - - - is "to be" then this will be followed by a - - - - .

SOLUTION ONE

The complete system of a language is called its *grammar*. This system uses words and arranges them in order, and this order is called *syntax*. The various patterns which these words form are combined to make sentences, and the words in these sentences can be allocated to various parts of speech or *word classes*.

The word, or group of words, which begins the sentence is called the *subject* of the sentence. The *subject* of a sentence, in English, is normally followed by a *verb*. If the *verb* is "to be", then this will be followed by a *complement*.

OUTLINE TWO

In the commonest kind of sentence, the typical pattern is a subject, followed by a verb, followed by the - - - - . This - - - - is normally a - - - - or - - - - group. We call these kinds of verbs - - - - verbs.

Verbs can be used in the past, present, or future. In other words, they have three basic - - - - s. And these three basic - - - - s can be further subdivided.

SOLUTION TWO

In the commonest kind of sentence, the typical pattern is a subject, followed by a verb, followed by the *object*. This *object* is normally a *noun* or *noun* group. We call these

161

kinds of verbs *transitive* verbs.

Verbs can be used in the past, present, or future. In other words, they have three basic *tenses*. And these three basic *tenses* can be further subdivided.

OUTLINE THREE

In a complex sentence, words form into groups. When a separate group of words contains a main verb, we call it a - - - - . If there is no main verb, the group of words will be a - - - - .

The most important group of words with a main verb in the sentence will be the - - - - - - - - . The groups of words which are dependent on this group of words but which also contain a main verb will be - - - - - - - - s.

SOLUTION THREE

In a complex sentence, words form into groups. When a separate group of words contains a main verb, we call it a *clause*. If there is no main verb, the group of words will be a *phrase*.

The most important group of words with a main verb in the sentence will be the *main clause*. The groups of words which are dependent on this group of words but which also contain a main verb will be *subordinate clauses*.

OUTLINE FOUR

There are seven main word classes in English: - - - - , - - - - , - - - - , - - - - , - - - - , - - - - , - - - - . The phrases and clauses in a sentence can also be classified more or less according to these same classes.

Some of these words will have special endings, called - - - - , according to their grammatical function. Sometimes, these endings will show grammatical agreement, or - - - - . Nouns are not classified into male, female, or neuter in English. In other words, they don't have a given - - - - . But nouns are marked for number. In other words, they are either - - - - or - - - - .

SOLUTION FOUR

There are seven main word classes in English: *nouns*, *verbs*, *adjectives*, *adverbs*, *prepositions*, *conjunctions*, and *pronouns*.

Some of these words will have special endings, called *inflections*, according to their grammatical function. Sometimes these endings will show grammatical agreement, or *concord*. Nouns are not classified into male, female, or neuter in English. In other words, they don't have a given *gender*. But nouns are marked for number. In other words, they are either *singular* or *plural*.

OUTLINE FIVE

The most useful way to look at words is according to the work that they do: their - - - - . Single adjectives, adjective phrases, and adjective clauses will all have an - - - - function. Words or groups of words which tell us more about the verb will have an - - - - function. Words which are grouped together to make subjects or objects will have a - - - - function.

SOLUTION FIVE

The most useful way to look at words is according to the work that they do: their *function*. Single adjectives, adjective phrases, and adjective clauses will all have an *adjectival* function. Words or groups of words which tell us more about the verb will have an *adverbial* function. Words which are grouped together to make subjects or objects will have a *nominal* function.

OUTLINE SIX

Certain words in sentences form a - - - - class: they cannot be added to. - - - - s and - - - - s form such classes. Nouns, on the other hand, are an - - - - class.

Words which simply show relationships between groups of words and which bind sentences or parts of sentences together are sometimes called - - - - words.

SOLUTION SIX

Certain words in sentences form a *closed* class: they cannot be added to. *Prepositions* and *conjunctions* form such classes. Nouns, on the other hand, are an *open* class.

Words which simply show relationships between groups of words and which bind sentences or parts of sentences together are sometimes called *structural* words.

OUTLINE SEVEN

The various word classes, with the exception of conjunctions, can be expanded into phrases and clauses. But whereas nominals and adjectivals cannot be subdivided into types, adverbials can be subdivided into seven major types: - - - - , - - - - , - - - - , - - - - , - - - - , - - - - , - - - - . These adverbials are often introduced by - - - - s like "in" or "to".

SOLUTION SEVEN

The various word classes, with the exception of conjunctions, can be expanded into phrases and clauses. But whereas nominals and adjectivals cannot be subdivided into types, adverbials can be subdivided into seven major types: *manner, time, place, frequency, condition, reason, result*. These adverbials are often introduced by *prepositions* like "in" or "to".

OUTLINE EIGHT

The study of the sounds in a language is called - - - - . This includes the rise and fall of words and groups of words (- - - -) and the strength given to parts of words or words in sentences (- - - -). Words are divided up into - - - - .

The letters of the alphabet should not be regarded as sounds, but as written letters. To describe the actual sounds of a language we need a list of symbols (called - - - -) and a - - - - alphabet. Then we can translate what we hear into a - - - - - - - - .

SOLUTION EIGHT

The study of the sounds in a language is called *phonetics*. This includes the rise and fall of words and groups of words (*intonation*) and the strength given to parts of words or words in sentences (*stress*). Words are divided up into *syllables*.

The letters of the alphabet should not be regarded as sounds, but as written letters. To describe the actual sounds of a language we need a list of symbols (called *phonemes*) and a *phonetic* alphabet. Then we can translate what we hear into a *phonetic transcription*.

OUTLINE NINE

English is composed of different - - - - s of the same language. These - - - - s are older versions of the language we now speak. Today, they are little more than regional ways of pronouncing words (- - - - s) but originally they were full languages with their own - - - - , or vocabulary, and their own syntax and grammar.

Nowadays, there is a form of the language called - - - - English, which developed from the form of the language once spoken in London. This form of writing and speaking the language makes nationwide and international communication easier and more efficient.

SOLUTION NINE

English is composed of different *dialects* of the same language. These *dialects* are older versions of the language we now speak. Today, they are little more than regional ways of pronouncing words (*accents*) but originally they were full languages with their own *lexis*, or vocabulary, and their own syntax and grammar.

Nowadays, there is a form of the language called *standard* English, which developed from the form of the language once spoken in London. This form of writing and speaking the language makes nationwide and international communication easier and more efficient.

OUTLINE TEN

It is useful to think of a sentence as a basic structure composed of a subject, a verb, and an object. Sometimes, it is useful to be able to separate the rest of the sentence from the subject, in which case we call the rest of the sentence the - - - - .

A simple sentence of this type can be built into a - - - - sentence by the process of changing or - - - - the different elements in the sentence. These changes can occur before the word or phrase (- - - -) or after it (- - - -).

SOLUTION TEN

It is useful to think of a sentence as a basic structure composed of a subject, a verb, and an object. Sometimes, it is useful to be able to separate the rest of the sentence from the subject, in which case we call the rest of the sentence the *predicate*.

A simple sentence of this type can be built into a *complex* sentence by the process of changing or *modifying* the different elements in the sentence. These changes can occur before the word or phrase (*premodification*) or after it (*postmodification*).

OUTLINE ELEVEN

Verb systems can be extremely complicated. To make description more effective, each verb - - - - is divided into - - - - persons, using pronouns. Three of these are singular and three are - - - - .

The past, present, and future - - - - s are further subdivided. In addition to this, the main verbs are modified by helping or - - - - verbs. Some of these verbs are referred to as - - - - , because they do not have a complete set of forms.

SOLUTION ELEVEN

Verb systems can be extremely complicated. To make description more effective, each verb *tense* is divided into *six* persons, using pronouns. Three of these are singular and three are *plural*.

The past, present, and future *tenses* are further subdivided. In addition to this, the main verbs are modified by helping or *auxiliary* verbs. Some of these verbs are referred to as *modals*, because they do not have a complete set of forms.

OUTLINE TWELVE

Each tense of the verb has a completed or - - - - form and an "-ing" form, referred to as a - - - - or - - - - . These forms are regarded for descriptive purposes as separate tenses.

To make these extra tenses, two main verbs are used as - - - - verbs, and it is these combinations which make the tenses. The helping verbs used are the verbs "- - - -" and "- - - -", and past, present, and future forms of these verbs are used in the combinations.

SOLUTION TWELVE

Each tense of the verb has a completed or *perfect* form and an "-ing" form, referred to as a *continuous* or *progressive*. These forms are regarded for descriptive purposes as separate tenses.

To make these extra tenses, two main verbs are used as *auxiliary* verbs, and it is these combinations which make the tenses. The helping verbs used are the verbs "*be*" and "*have*", and past, present, and future forms of these verbs are used in the combinations.

OUTLINE THIRTEEN

The verb tenses are used to describe time, and this can be rather abstract. For instance, we can talk about something which "will have happened", using the - - - - - - - - tense, or something that "had been happening" (- - - - - - - - - - - -) when something else "happened" (- - - - - - - -), or "was happening" (- - - - - - - -). We can even use extra helping verbs (- - - - - - - - s) to say things like: "He might have been cleaning the car when the bomb went off". In this case, we have a - - - - - - - - - - - - tense, modified by the past form of the modal verb "- - - - ".

SOLUTION THIRTEEN

The verb tenses are used to describe time, and this can be rather abstract. For instance, we can talk about something which "will have happened", using the *future perfect* tense, or something that "had been happening" (*past perfect continuous* or *progressive*) when something else "happened" (*past simple*), or "was happening" (*past continuous* or *progressive*). We can even use extra helping verbs (*modal auxiliaries*) to say things like: "He might have been cleaning the car when the bomb went off". In this case, we have a *present perfect continuous* tense, modified by the past form of the modal verb "may".

OUTLINE FOURTEEN

Verbs are divided into two groups according to whether they behave in a normal or an unusual way. Normal verbs are termed - - - - , while the others are regarded as - - - - . Any abnormality is most noticeable in the - - - - simple tense.

The "ing" form of the verb is called the - - - - participle. There is an "-ed" form in the past called the - - - - - - - - . This form, too, is different in - - - - - - - - s.

SOLUTION FOURTEEN

Verbs are divided into two groups according to whether they behave in a normal or an unusual way. Normal verbs are termed *regular*, while the others are regarded as *irregular*. Any abnormality is most noticeable in the *past* simple tense.

The "ing" form of the verb is called the *present* participle. There is an "-ed" participle form called the *past participle*. This form, too, is different in *irregular verbs*.

OUTLINE FIFTEEN

Verbs which are composed of more than one word are called - - - - word verbs. The words which are added to a main verb form to make the verb are called - - - - . These may be adverbs or prepositions. When these verbs are unbreakable wholes, they can be called - - - - verbs. Each of these wholes is regarded as a complete verb and receives its own entry in a dictionary.

The grammar of these verbs is complex and there is some disagreement over definition. A - - - - approach, or analysis according to meaning, is often helpful in these cases. The verb "take", for example, has no - - - - connection with the phrasal verb "take off" when "take off" means "leave the ground".

SOLUTION FIFTEEN

Verbs which are composed of more than one word are called *multi* word verbs. The words which are added to a main verb form to make the verb are called *particles*. These may be adverbs or prepositions. When these verbs are unbreakable wholes, they can be called *phrasal* verbs. Each of these wholes is regarded as a complete verb and receives its own entry in a dictionary.

The grammar of these verbs is complex and there is some disagreement over definition. A *semantic* approach, or analysis according to meaning, is often helpful in these cases. The verb "take", for example, has no *semantic* connection with the phrasal verb "take off" when "take off" means "leave the ground".

OUTLINE SIXTEEN

There is a connection between verbs and other word classes via the participles. The - - - - - - - - can be used to form nouns ending in "-ing", for example, and the - - - - - - - - can be used to form adjectives ending in "-ed".

Many - - - - can be formed from adjectives by adding "-ly". And both adjectives and - - - - s have special comparative and - - - - forms. Sometimes these forms consist of

one word, but sometimes they are made by adding
"- - - -" or "- - - -".

SOLUTION SIXTEEN
There is a connection between verbs and other word
classes via the participles. The *present participle* can be
used to form nouns ending in "-ing", for example, and the
past participle can be used to form adjectives ending in
"-ed".

Many *adverbs* can be formed from adjectives by adding
"-ly". And both adjectives and *adverbs* have special
comparative and *superlative* forms. Sometimes these forms
consist of one word, but sometimes they are made by
adding "*more*" or "*most*".

OUTLINE SEVENTEEN
- - - - are important because they show the relationship
between two nouns, especially positional and spatial relations. They are a - - - - class and are often used to construct
- - - - s, like "in the kitchen". When they are formed from
more than one word, like "on top of", they are called
- - - - - - - - s.

SOLUTION SEVENTEEN
Prepositions are important because they show the relationship between two nouns, especially positional and spatial
relations. They are a *closed* class and are often used to
construct *adverbials*, like "in the kitchen". When they are
formed from more than one word, like "on top of", they
are called *complex prepositions*.

OUTLINE EIGHTEEN
- - - - s or linking words can be simple, as in "and" and
- - - -, as in "as soon as". The linking function of "as
soon as", to take one example, is very subtle. Such subtle
linking is also apparent in blocks of language, called - - - -,

where the way everything holds together is called - - - - .

Where a linking word in no way alters the grammar of a sentence and operates above this level, we call such a word a - - - - - - - -

SOLUTION EIGHTEEN
Conjunctions or linking words can be simple, as in "and" and *complex*, as in "as soon as". The linking function of "as soon as", to take one example, is very subtle. Such subtle linking is also apparent in blocks of language, called *text*, where the way everything holds together is called *cohesion*.

Where a linking word in no way alters the grammar of a sentence and operates above this level, we call such a word a *sentence connector*.

OUTLINE NINETEEN
Written language requires certain marks to be added to increase the effectiveness of communication. These marks are called - - - - . Such marks are used to show where sentences end (- - - - - - - - s) and where words or groups of words should be separated (- - - - s). To group items together in a long list, - - - - - - - - s can be used. Other kinds of separation (as in this case) can be shown by round or square - - - - s or by - - - - s. Spoken language is shown by using - - - - - - - - s and possession or the omission of letters in a word by - - - - s.

SOLUTION NINETEEN
Written language requires certain marks to be added to increase the effectiveness of communication. These marks are called *punctuation*. Such marks are used to show where sentences end (*full-stops*) and where words or groups of words should be separated (*commas*). To group items together in a long list, *semi-colons* can be used. Other kinds of separation (as in this case) can be shown by round or square *brackets* or by *dashes*. Spoken language is shown

by using *quotation marks* and possession or the omission of letters in a word by *apostrophes*.

OUTLINE TWENTY
The study of textual cohesion and such matters comes under the blanket term - - - - - - - - . This, like grammar, is part of - - - - . The specialised study of different kinds of text, whether spoken or written, is termed - - - - . When such a study is confined to literary texts, we speak of - - - - - - - - . But this tends to be more concerned with content and outside reference than with the text itself.

The study of back reference (- - - -), forward reference (- - - -) and other forms of textual construction and cohesion are, however, always necessary if we are to determine the nature of what is there on the paper, whether this is regarded as literature or not.

SOLUTION TWENTY
The study of textual cohesion and such matters comes under the blanket term *discourse analysis*. This, like grammar, is part of *linguistics*. The specialised study of different kinds of text, whether spoken or written, is termed *stylistics*. When such a study is confined to literary texts, we speak of *literary criticism*. But this tends to be more concerned with content and outside reference than with the text itself.

The study of back reference (*anaphora*), forward reference (*cataphora*) and other forms of textual construction and cohesion are, however, always necessary if we are to determine the nature of what is there on the paper, whether this is regarded as literature or not.

OUTLINE TWENTY-ONE
Language should be seen as a whole. Its rule-governed system, or - - - - , and its sound system, or phonology, come together to make a complex phenomenon. To understand all this, some knowledge of elementary language

science, or - - - - is helpful, and a basic knowledge of
- - - - terminology is necessary. We cannot talk about
houses, cars, cooking, or football without knowing the
- - - - , or vocabulary, that belongs to them. The same goes
for language.

SOLUTION TWENTY-ONE

Language should be seen as a whole. Its rule-governed
system, or *grammar*, and its sound system, or phonology,
come together to make a complex phenomenon. To understand all this, some knowledge of elementary language
science, or *linguistics* is helpful, and a basic knowledge of
grammatical terminology is necessary. We cannot talk
about houses, cars, cooking, or football without knowing
the *lexis*, or vocabulary, that belongs to them. The same
goes for language.

16

Making Mistakes

We all make mistakes, and this is especially so with the language that we speak and write. The question is: How important are these mistakes? Do they matter?

In one sense, all mistakes matter. Language, looked at in this way, is no different from a game. In a game, we know – or are told by an umpire or referee – when we break a rule, and we are normally penalised for our offence. We also know when we've made a mistake. Perhaps, we hit the ball with the edge of the racket, or sliced the golf drive.

But all of us play whatever games we play with varying degrees of skill. A tiny minority gets a place in the national team, or even reaches anything near that level. For the rest of us, we play because we are intrigued by the difficulties, or are very competitive, or just for the fun of it.

It's not entirely a game

With our mother tongue it's rather different. It's sometimes a game, of course. We joke, tell stories, and argue. We do these things to impress people, make them laugh, prove ourselves superior, and so on. But we wouldn't think of being anti-social enough to spoil stories and jokes by pointing out what we thought were pronunciation and grammar mistakes.

''Well, me and him, Jack there, we was walking down Oxford Street like, and we see this bloke coming down the other way, other side of the street like. Yeah. Right. And this bloke, see, he's walking along like with something in his ear. In his ear. Right. And you know what that was? In his ear? That was a bloody banana. Right. So Jack, right, being a bit of a lad like, he calls out, see. 'Hey, mate,' he shouts like. 'You got a bloody banana in your ear, mate.' And this bloke, see, he looks over and he sees Jack like shouting and waving his arms. And you know what he shouts, this bloke? He shouts, 'Can't hear you mate. I got a bloody banana in my ear.' "

We don't want to spoil the joke. There's the chance of a laugh, and we want to encourage the speaker to tell the joke as best he or she can. We enter into the spirit of the thing. This is communication. And the test of the joke is partly how well it's told. Provided the joke's a good one, the best communication will, usually, produce the most laughter. How often we've heard people say, "It's not the joke. It's the way you tell it." Perhaps you yourself are one of those people who can't tell jokes: you remember the story-line, but you can't bring the story to life.

All this tells us a lot about language. Indeed, much of this kind of thing is studied in that aspect of language we call *sociolinguistics*. Sociolinguists study language in its social contexts. If you think about it, language is always manifest in some kind of social context. We speak our language with friends, family, at work, and wherever we congregate with other people.

When we are at play, as it were, we are not at work. When we are at the office, we tend to use a different kind of language from the language we use at the pub. We use a different *register*. Our language at the office will tend to be in a more formal register than our language at the pub.

If our joke about the banana had been told in a formal register, and with a non-regional pronunciation, then it might have fallen a bit flat. For the joke to have been a success, the story-teller would have had to speak in an informal register and with, preferably, a regional accent. Most of the comedians you hear and watch on television have strong regional accents, and that is part of their success. They appear totally fluent and well in control of their material.

This isn't to say that what is sometimes called a "posh" accent isn't used in comedy. Of course it is. But the accent is used in a mocking way, and often as a contrast to other ways of speaking. In that sense, there are strong possibilities for comedy in a comedian exaggerating what used to be called an "upper class" or "Oxford" accent.

Fluency

The question of fluency is most important. If you walk through a street market and stop to listen to street-traders shouting their wares, you are listening to professionals. Linger for any length of time in front of a stall where a crowd has begun to gather and you will hear the language at its most fluent, amusing, and persuasive. This is language of a very high order. But what about mistakes?

So what is a mistake?

The more this question of mistakes crops up in the many social situations where language is used, the more the very idea seems incongruous. The fact is, people speaking their mother tongue, like you and me, don't really make mistakes. We make mistakes when we speak a foreign language, but not when we speak our own.

You will probably disagree strongly with what I've just written. You are convinced that you make a lot of mistakes in English, and you are convinced that some of your friends do, too. Just as you are equally convinced that other friends speak really good English. But what do you mean?

Early on in this book, I set out to show that most of the trouble with language study, and especially the study of grammar, is our own lack of self-confidence. It all seems so complicated and quite beyond us. I hope that, by now, your own confidence has considerably increased. I hope that you are much surer of your ability to absorb the terminology and understand what it means.

You know enough now to realise, if you give it some thought, that you could use all the grammar that we've talked about in this book, even if you didn't know the names for the different parts and what they did. If you still don't believe me, look at this paragraph:

"If done through he what how horse after that we well know absorb. That lack own are this if did how not names believe paragraph book use if. That at much I terminology to."

You would never write anything like this. But, in order *not* to write something like this, you need to know your grammar. And the amount of grammar which comes into play to write three fairly complex English sentences is enormous. As you now well know. But what you've forgotten is that you really do know it. You know it because you can do it. If you have ever listened to yourself recorded on tape and speaking with confidence in a normal social situation, you should have been really impressed. But, of course, you weren't. Why not? Because you were convinced that your accent was horrible and that you were speaking bad English and making mistakes.

I'm sorry, but you've got to start from what you *can* do, not from what you think you can't. You *can* speak your own language, when you don't think about it too much, with wonderful fluency. You speak it with a fluency which is the envy of almost every foreigner worldwide who is trying to learn to speak it better. Never forget that.

Yet you still insist that you make a lot of mistakes. The question is, if they are mistakes, what kinds of mistakes are they?

As soon as you begin to think about these so-called mistakes, you make reference not to your spoken English but your written English. You think of all those pieces of writing you did when you were at school, and all that red ink. There were so many mistakes.

If you care to think back to those painful times, you will find that most of those mistakes were to do with spelling, punctuation, paragraphing, and things like that. Almost none of them were to do with grammar. Admittedly, there were sentences which the teacher underlined because they were not clear. But these poorly expressed sentences were probably carelessly written, rather than ungrammatical. Maybe you repeated words or left words out. On the other hand, you may have been so worried about the whole thing that you lost all confidence in displaying your linguistic skills.

Custom and convention

As we learned very early on in this book, things like spelling and punctuation are matters of custom and convention. They fully belong to the written language, too. And there lies the nub. It's not so much a matter of grammar as a matter of learning what the convention is. When we speak our language, we bring into play a huge complex of language skills, and we all do that very well. But when we write our language, we are doing something which is relatively artificial. And to translate what we can do in speaking into the medium of writing is much more difficult.

Let's leave this business of writing for a moment, and go back to speaking. You are, by now, well aware that there is a standard form of spoken English and various regional forms. People normally show where they come from by having a local accent. Some people, however, have either been educated and trained to speak without a local accent, or have themselves decided to speak with more of a standard pronunciation. There is still one kind of accent which marks a person out as coming from a major English public school, although it is possible for someone to learn such an accent by a process of careful imitation. Most people would regard what might still be called a 'public school accent' as "affected". By that, they mean that the accent seems unreal, unnatural, and "put on". It is also seen to convey a sense of superiority, and an elitism which is scornful of those whose accents are not marked in the same way.

Those of us who don't speak with that kind of accent and find it affected, nevertheless feel that people who speak like that don't make mistakes. For various reasons, they make us feel inferior. If anybody's going to make mistakes, it's us. Even if that kind of accent has been modified to become more natural and less marked, we still

feel that what is being spoken is the right kind of English –
or "proper" English, as people used to say.

Regional dialects

Let's turn the tables. Let's imagine someone with a public
school accent trying to speak one of the regional dialects. I
think we would find such an attempt ludicrous. If you are a
good mimic, it is possible to have a reasonable shot at it.
But to speak in a regional dialect for any length of time,
and in many different social situations, calls for an intimate
knowledge of that particular form of the language. We are,
once again, talking of linguistic skills of a very high order.
Even *dialectologists* (people who have studied particular
dialects for years) are unable to do this well, unless the
dialect is their own.

Now, the person with a public school accent who is
trying to speak a dialect, but speaking it badly, really *is*
making mistakes. There's no doubt about that whatsoever.
If that person is putting an "s" on the third person singular
while attempting to speak in Norfolk dialect, that person is
making a grammatical mistake. If that person puts the
aspirate (the "h" sound) at the beginning of words which
are spelt with the letter "h" when he is trying to speak
'cockney', that person is making a pronunciation mistake.
It cannot be too strongly emphasised that English dialects
have their own grammatical rules and their own phonology.

The problems really begin when we move from our own
dialect and try to speak the standard, because the standard
form of the language is so much more artificial. When we
try to speak the standard form and obey all the other
conventions and customs when we write it, our difficulties
are compounded. For those brought up, or educated, to
speak standard English, the difficulties of writing it are far
less than for those who weren't. But, because the standard
form is related to the various dialects, it isn't all that
unfamiliar.

Fortunately, it isn't customary to write in dialect. Some
writers do, of course, and there are some writers who make

a habit of doing so, for various reasons. Books in dialect sell well in the areas where that particular dialect is spoken, for obvious reasons. And certain poets – like the Dorset poet William Barnes and the Scottish poet Robert Burns – are chiefly remembered for their dialect poems. However, if you've ever tried to read Burns or Barnes in the original and happen to speak neither of their dialects, you will have found it hard going.

Because we don't write in our own dialect, we stand no chance of mixing the written dialect with written standard English. Our own dialect grammar will normally require little modification for it to become acceptable standard written English. There will be the odd "local" mistake but, as I've said, most of our mistakes will be in the areas of spelling and punctuation. Most of the English dialects drop the "h" at the beginning of words, but this is almost unheard of in writing.

However, since written English does belong to the standard form, people who are strong dialect speakers and have a strong sense of local identity are intimidated by it. Indeed, this is what causes many problems when some public officials are interviewed on the radio or TV. The attempt to shift into standard English from their own local form of English becomes quite noticeable. The more uncomfortable they are, the more uncertain they become of how exactly to say what they have to say.

It cannot be too strongly stressed that our own natural fluency in our own language will be seriously interrupted if we become too conscious of what we are saying. We really do have to believe that it will come out right. And it is much more likely to come out right if we leave things alone than if we think about getting our grammar right. The mental processes which are going on when we use our language are so complex that the greatest experts are only just beginning to understand them. If we think about what we are saying, we are thinking in the same language that we are speaking but at a lower and clumsier level. The two processes do not mix well. One involves enormously complex natural skills, and the other involves knowledge which is fairly basic and limited.

To speak and write well depends very much on not being too self-conscious. The natural fluency in speaking, which all but a very few people possess, should not be interfered with too much. It is, if you like, a precious gift which we all naturally develop. If we are confident enough to be happy with our local accent in all social situations, our spoken English will be so much the more easy and fluent. If we meddle too much and try to speak in what feels like a foreign way, we shall lose fluency and competence, not gain it.

The aim is effective communication. For that, we need the whole range of language which we naturally inherit. If we are to behave naturally in the wide variety of social situations which confront us in life, we have to have confidence in our inheritance.

Written English

With written English, things are, as I've said, rather different. But not too different. Although written English may appear to some of us rather difficult, the more we write, the more we should feel happier about writing well. After all, this is still our language, albeit an unusual form of it.

But however well we learn the rules of spelling and punctuation – and they are not really all that difficult to learn – using language still remains a skill which we possess in varying degrees. Although all of us are remarkably fluent when we are speaking our language, and many of us are remarkably fluent when we write it, the actual levels of skill vary from individual to individual.

We are not talking about mistakes here, and this is where much of the confusion arises. It's not a matter of making mistakes or not. It is a matter of confidence and natural gifts. We can all increase our speaking and writing skills, but we shall still be less fluent and skilful than lots of other people.

Well, what about standards then? What sort of level of correctness should we be aiming at? What about all this talk about literacy and literacy levels?

There is no proven connection between knowledge of

grammar and speaking and writing ability. We can learn as much about English grammar as we like or are made to learn, but there is no guarantee that such knowledge will improve our English. Speaking and writing are skills. Knowledge is of quite a different order.

Consider our game of tennis again. There are numerous people who write about tennis for a living and have an encyclopaedic knowledge of the game, but whose tennis-playing skills are very average. There are lots of people who know everything there is to know about motor cars but who drive them very badly. The same goes for all kinds of activities which involve skills. Hours and hours of learning about English grammar will have little or no effect on our ability to speak and write fluently. The reverse is more likely the case. The more we become self-conscious about these matters, the more inhibited we are likely to become.

So, let's relegate the problem of making mistakes to where it belongs: rather low in our list of priorities. What we should aim at is confidence, naturalness, sympathetic interaction with other people, and the real wish to communicate our thoughts, feelings, and opinions as effectively as possible. If we concentrate on these, the problem of correctness will solve itself.

Finally, there are no revision exercises at the end of this chapter, but here are the new terms we have met:

New Grammatical Terms (16)
dialectology the study of dialects
register the type of language used to suit the occasion
sociolinguistics the study of language in social contexts

17

Exercises

Basics (answers on page 225)

1. Which of these words are verbs and which are adverbs?
    find; easily; quickly; run; running; fast; slowly; slide; carry; calmly.

2. Underline the stressed syllable in these words:
    after; impossible; correct; marry; underline; forecast; courageously; dinner; musical; similar.

3. Correct the syntax in these phrases:
    in end the; for the being time; the house big; is here the car; the moon over; high dry and; the one the end at; when came the time; there not; it take or it leave.

4. How many vowel letters are there in each of these words?
    afternoon; watch; settee; piece; house; football; guard; news; marmalade; cheese.

5. How many consonants are there in those words?

6. How many vowel sounds are there in those words?

7. Which of these pairs have the same pronunciation?
see/sea; peer/pear; where/were; there/their; here/hear; hair/hare; saw/sore; pine/pane; rain/rein; pry/prey.

8. How many tenses of the verb *come* are there in this sentence?
When he came to the shore the waves were coming in so fast that the boat that comes every Friday had already come into harbour.

9. Two of these sentences have the same intonation. Which are they?
He stood and waited. Where were they? They weren't usually late. Was the train late? Then he saw them. Was that John with them?

10. Change these phrases to show concord:
the clock say five; all man are equal; nine apple; time fly; he is washing herself; those is their bags; these is it; the soldier are coming; take these present home; Mary and Jane is sister.

11. Underline the inflections in these words:
horses; cows; singing; their; mine; races; parties; lazy; footballers; caught

Nuts and Bolts (answers on page 226)

1. Which of these are nouns?
woman; nice; tidy; children; toast; windy; rough; car; policeman; teacher

2. Which of these are abstract nouns?
table; silence; water; cheese; friendship; fear; hunger; food; night; darkness

3. Which of these are concrete nouns?
mother; mood; tea; student; learning; window; wisdom; anger; angel; love

4. Which of these are adjectives?
   ground; large; comfortable; comfort; bush; breeze;
   warm; dizzy; law; muddy

5 What parts of speech are the following words?
   lovely; yellow; quickly; misery; usefully; utility;
   strange; tidily; horse; nature

6. Which of these are in the past?
   yesterday; likes; today; tomorrow; went; married;
   now; saw; eat; studied

7. Which of these are in the present?
   this morning; last night; every day; buys; cycling;
   before; at present; jumps; hello; sleeps

8. Which of these are sentences?
   (a) *before the holidays*
   (b) *and after that*
   (c) *He never ever*
   (d) *Watch this space.*
   (e) *Silence is golden but*
   (f) *I saw him in the shop yesterday morning.*
   (g) *before the weather became so bad that I*
       couldn't
   (h) *Yes, I do.*
   (i) *Come into the garden with me and see*
   (j) *came into the garden with me.*

Sorting Things Out (answers on page 226)
1. What gender are these words?
   table; girl; waitress; hero; emperor; queen; vixen;
   dinner; tree

2. Group these words into their correct grammatical
   category (for example, nice, pretty, clean; fish, cow,
   house):
   is; grammar; readers; interesting; enjoyable; sub-
   ject; return

3. Which of these are impersonal?
your; trees; economics; John's; their; the nation's; mine; China

4. Which of these show number?
lovely; hopeful; prayers; a car; crowded; crowds; red; roses; litres

5. Which of these are objects?
Jenny hit the ball; the storm destroyed the houses; Arsenal won the cup

6. Which of these are personal?
milk; cheese; Mary; rain; her; she; laughing; police- man; boat

7. How many phonemes are there in these words?
bought; bike; laughing; motor; hill; light; mine

8. Which of these are plural?
car; planes; they; light; soldiers; shield; arches; hope

9. Which of these are possessives?
their; father's; lorries; birds; her; William's; noses; buses

10. Underline the prefixes in these words:
indirect; punish; polecat; undo; upturn; outgoing; onset; postscript

11. Which of these are pronouns?
he; Maria; their; there; eye; I; his; ourselves; it

12. Which is the semantic part of this sentence?
The word 'defend' means 'protect from harm'.

13. Which of these are singular?
peach; laughter; files; status; series; codes; crowd; pie; pieces

14. Which of these is standard pronunciation?
    laughter: larfter or laffter; their: thurr or theyer; isn't it: innit or iznit

15. Which are the subjects in these sentences?
    Cats eat fish. Cheese tastes very nice. You are welcome. I swim.

Parts of the Sentence (answers on page 227)

1. Can you identify the adverbial in this sentence?
   He worked hard all afternoon.

2. Which is the adverbial phrase in this sentence?
   She ran the marathon with great courage and tenacity.

3. How many articles are there in this sentence?
   William took the book and placed it on the table where a large pile of books had already been dumped.

4. How many clauses are there in this sentence?
   The plane circled the airport twice and, after landing, it taxied down the runway.

5. Can you identify the complement in this sentence?
   Julia felt as if she was about to be sick.

6. Which of these sentences is complex?
   Henry waited. It was dark and eerie. He took the torch from his pocket with very great care. Then he switched it on and saw a man who was running away from the car. It was Jimmy Walton.

7. Which of these two sentences is a compound sentence?
   Some liked the idea but some hated it.
   Some liked the idea as much as the others.

8. How many conjunctions are there in this sentence and what are they?
    Jack and Jill went up the hill to fetch a pail of water, but the well at the top was dry so they had to go on to the next village and ask an old lady if they could use her well instead.

9. There are co-ordinate clauses in one of these sentences. Which one?
    We went to our mother's for tea. When she opened the door she was so pleased to see us she cried out, "What a lovely surprise!" Then she asked us inside and told us to sit down. It's such a beautiful cottage. We both love it so much.

10. Can you identify the diphthongs in these words?
    paint; idea; pint; theoretical; mysterious; boys; boisterous

11. Can you identify the homonyms?
    piper, paper; riper, reaper; line, line; hear, hear; tear, tear

12. Which is the main clause in this sentence?
    After a few moments of quiet reflection, Jack walked slowly towards the burglar, without saying anything and without doing anything which might anger him.

13. Which of the following are monosyllabic words?
    driver; car; exhaust; bonnet; axle; windscreen; door; boot; wiper

14. How many morphemes are there in the following word?
    learning

15. Which are the phrases in this sentence?
    At one o'clock exactly, Tim caught the train to London, having promised his father, very seriously, that he wouldn't be late back.

16. How many polysyllabic words are there here?
   night; daylight; friend; friendship; seldom; bright; courtesy; waste

17. Can you identify the predicate in this sentence?
   The lady with the large red hat standing near the station clock is my mother.

18. Which are the prepositional phrases in the following sentence?
   I love fishing, especially at night or with my best friend, Ted.

19. Which of these are prepositions?
   how; on; by; why; in; at; again; where; if; it

Building the Sentence (answers on page 228)

1. Can you identify the adjective clause in this sentence?
   My next-door neighbour has a small cat which loves creamy milk.

2. In the following paragraph, there are five types of adverb. Identify the adverbs and say which type they are:
   Yesterday, I went to my favourite market. I often go there on Saturdays. While I was there I bought a lot of vegetables.

3. Write down the common nouns in these sentences:
   Cows eat grass. Daisy, my father's cow, likes newly mown hay. She munches it slowly. Our farm is called 'Home Farm' and we have lived in the same house for years.

4. Which of the following nouns are countable?
   sheep; dog; milk; water; bird; cow; air; rice

5. Pick out the definite and indefinite articles in this passage, and write them down:

It was a long day. The train seemed to stop at every station. At Manchester, some soldiers got onto the train. They kept shouting and, in the end, the ticket collector told them to be quiet.

6. Which are the demonstratives here?
   Which one is yours? Is it this one or that one? Those are Jean's and these are Bill's. That means that that one over there belongs to you.

7. Underline the determiners:
   All men are equal, but some men are more equal than others.

8, Which part of this sentence is finite and which is non-finite?
   Imagine going home, to sit by the fire, to sleep in the warm; but I needed to continue my journey.

9. Which are the infinitives in the above sentence?

10. Which is the noun clause in this sentence, and which is the noun phrase?
    A rich but disappointed man, he still loved the money he had earned.

Expanding the Parts (answers on page 229)

1. Which is the adjunct in this sentence?
   She played the violin with wonderful sensitivity.

2. Can you identify the adverb clause of time in this sentence?
   The bell rang when the lesson had finished.

3. There are three adverbials in this passage. Can you find them?
   The door slowly opened and a figure emerged. He

*was wearing a mask and holding a gun. Suddenly, a
shot rang out. When the smoke had cleared, the man
lay dead.*

4. Which are the intransitive verbs in this sentence?
   *After walking for about ten hours he was exhausted.
   He took his jacket and laid it on the ground. It was
   exactly ten o'clock and very dark. But the ground was
   warm. He closed his eyes and slept. Six hours later,
   he awoke.*

5. Write down the two examples of modification in this
   sentence:
   *The man with dark hair pushed the little boy onto the
   bus.*

6. Which is the postmodifier here?
   *The house painted white is where my little Polish
   grandmother lived.*

7. Which is the premodifier in this sentence?
   *My little Polish grandmother loved the house where
   she lived.*

8. Can you identify the two subordinate clauses in this
   sentence?
   *When the rain had stopped, we went into the garden,
   which was in a sorry state.*

9. Which is the transitive verb in this sentence?
   *He hammered the nail into the wall and it seemed to
   hold.*

10. Can you say which word classes these belong to?
    fingers; beautiful; slowly; on; swim

The Importance of the Verb (answers on page 230)

1. Which are the auxiliary verbs here?
   I should like to come but I haven't finished my homework yet.

2. There is one contraction in the sentence above. Which is it?

3. Which verb is the copula in the sentence below?
   He looks as if he needs a drink.

4. Which word classes do these three words belong to?
   copular; copulative; copula

5. In which tense is the verb in this sentence?
   On Tuesday, I'll be twenty-two years old.

6. Which of the verbs in this sentence are helping verbs?
   I shall be travelling to London on Wednesday, but it will be quite late when I get back home so I shouldn't wait up for me if I were you.

7. Which of these verb forms are irregular?
   fished; fought; fried; found; freed; followed; felt

8. Write down the main verbs in this sentence:
   She could have passed easily but she didn't revise properly.

9. Which are the verb participles in the sentence below?
   She was running so fast that she had passed the mile mark ages before the others reached it.

10. Which is the past participle in the sentence above?

11. How many past tense forms are there in that sentence?

12. Can you identify the present continuous tense below?
    She's coming round the bend now and I think she's going to win.

13. Which are the present participles in this sentence?
    I'm leaving you because you're making my life a misery.

14. Can you identify the present simple tenses in this sentence?
    I like shopping but I don't like it as much as I like gardening.

15. How many examples of the present are there in this sentence, and what are they?
    The sky is going dark but the sun is still shining behind a cloud, but you can't say how the weather will turn out because it's so unpredictable, just like it was yesterday in fact.

16. Which one of the following verbs is irregular?
    was; drove; tried; left; sold; went

17. How many short forms are there in this sentence and which are they?
    I can't see you on Monday because I've got to see the doctor.

More About the Verb (answers on page 231)

1. Which of the verbs in this sentence is active?
   He was seen by several doctors but they weren't sure about him.

2. In the following paragraph, identify the tenses of the verbs:
   I'm trying to understand you. I've always tried to do that. I try all the time. In fact, I've been trying for years and I shall always try. I shall be trying in twenty years' time, I expect. In fact, in two years' time, I'll have been trying to understand you for ten years. I tried and tried. I always did. You know that. To think that in twenty years' time I'll have tried to understand you for twenty-eight years. I was trying to

193

understand you soon after we got married, just as I'd
tried to understand you before that. I'd always been
trying to understand you. You know that.

3. Because they are to do with 'time' what are all these
    verb tenses examples of?

4. What are their actual forms and the way these forms
    change examples of?

5. The paragraph above begins with the first person
    singular of the pronoun. Can you describe the pro-
    noun 'you' in a similar way?

6. How would you describe the pronoun 'we'?

7. In what form are the two verbs in the following
    sentence?
    Take it or leave it.

8. Which is the inflected form of the verb in the follow-
    ing sentence?
    To be or not to be, that is the question.

9. The form of the verbs in Question 7 expresses an
    'attitude'. What do we call that in grammatical termi-
    nology?

10. In the following sentence, identify the multi-word
    verb, in the negative, and identify the particles of that
    verb:
    Whatever his parents said, he certainly shouldn't
    have put up with it.

11. Can you passivise that sentence by first changing 'he'
    to 'it'?

12. Which of these verbs is in the active and which in the
    passive?
    It had to be tested and he tested it.

13. The kind of action described by the following verb form is referred to as what?
He's done it.

14. There is an 'ing' form tense in the following sentence, and this form can be described by another term. What is it?
He was laughing all the way to the bank.

15. There is an unusual subjunctive form of the verb in the following sentence. Can you identify it?
When I think about how successful you've been, I sometimes wish I were you.

16. There is a verbal group in the following passage which contains an uninflected two-word verb in the active voice. Can you find it?
Look, John. Whatever happens and in spite of everything we've experienced together, I'm absolutely sure we'll get by. I know we will. We always have.

17. Can you complete the following sentence?
The way in which people customarily speak and write a language is very important in linguistics, because it is this . . . which eventually determines what is correct and what is incorrect.

Adjectives and Description (answers on page 232)

1. In the sentence below, which adjectives are used attributively?
The little brown dog chased the white spotted ball.

2. Which of the adjectives in this sentence are comparatives?
He was taller than me, so I decided to move to a higher seat.

3. Can you identify the compound noun below?
   I was astonished: the income tax return was completely blank.

4. Which are the intensifiers in the sentences which follow?
   She was very lucky. Although the fire was extremely fierce, she managed to escape.

5. How many comparatives and how many nominals are there in the following passage?
   It was such a nice morning. In fact, it was even nicer than it was yesterday. The sun was shining more brightly than ever. I felt better than I had yesterday, too.

6. Can you identify the participial adjective in the sentence below?
   The broken window didn't bother me.

7. Which is the predicative adjective in the following sentence?
   The newly commissioned vessel fought the gathering storm.

8. Which is the subject complement in the following sentence?
   The ripe apples were red and crisp.

9. There are three superlative adjectives in the following passage. Can you identify them?
   It was the best holiday I'd ever had. It wasn't the cheapest either. But, it was certainly the hottest. The daily temperature was in the high thirties.

How Adverbs Can Help (answers on page 232)

1. Can you identify the adverb clause of condition in the following sentence?

   I'm quite happy to lend you my guide book if you promise to return it.

2. Which is the adverb clause of frequency in the following sentence?

   You can come and see me whenever you can find the time.

3. Which is the adverb clause of manner in the following sentence?

   She acted as if she owned the place.

4. Which is the adverb clause of place in the next sentence?

   We drove into town and parked where the old cinema used to be.

5. Which is the adverb clause of reason in the following sentence?

   I always enjoy fishing because it's so peaceful.

6. Which is the adverb clause of result in the following sentence?

   I got up very late in the morning so I missed the early train.

7. Which is the adverb clause of time in the following sentence?

   When the bells rang I knew it was time for the service.

8. Can you identify the adverb of manner in the next sentence?

   She opened the packet carefully in case she spilt any of the contents.

9. Put the adverbial in the next sentence in end position:

   Every Tuesday, we play tennis.

10. Put the adverbial in the following sentence in initial position:

    The gunman, very slowly and deliberately, fired two shots.

11. Put the adverbial in the next sentence in medial position:

    Of course, she is the college principal.

12. Which are the structural words in the following sentence?

    She laughed and suddenly, at that moment, John came into the room.

Tying Things Together: Prepositions (answers on page 233)

1. Which of the words in the following sentence belong to a closed class?

    Go to the shop and get me a bottle of milk.

2. Which is the complex preposition in the sentence below?

    Come into the shelter and get out of the rain.

3. Which of the words in the sentence below belong to an open class?

    We lived in a detached house with a large back garden.

4. Can you identify the phrasal prepositional verb in the following sentence?

    I simply will not put up with all this nonsense.

5. Which is the phrasal verb in the following sentence?

    The plane finally took off at about ten thirty.

6. Can you identify the prepositional complements in the next sentence?

    Will the people at the front please move to the back?

7. Which is the prepositional verb in the following sentence?
Make him comfortable and send for a doctor immediately.

8. Pick out the simple prepositions in the passage below:
I opened the door and went into the room. There was no-one there. An open book lay on a chair and there was an unfinished mug of coffee on the table. Near the table, lying on the floor, was a pair of carpet slippers. I walked quietly to the window and looked out. A man stood on the gravel drive looking steadily at me. It was Tom Watkins.

Joining Things Up: Conjunctions (answers on page 234)

1. Can you identify the adverbial conjunction in this sentence?
It wasn't her fault; nevertheless she was late.

2. Which of the words in the passage below give it cohesion?
You could say that. However, if you approach the subject from a different angle you will see the problem differently. It becomes much more complex. Therefore, on consideration, you will come to a different conclusion.

3. Can you pick out the complex conjunction in the following sentence?
She opened the box so that I could see inside.

4. Which is the conjunct in the sentence below?
She kept the box firmly closed. As a result, I was unable to see what was inside.

5. How many constituents are there in this sentence?
She kept the box firmly closed.

6. Which is the coordinating conjunction in the sentence below?
    She took out the key and she locked the door.

7. Which are the linking words in the following passage?
    That isn't what I said. What I said was that the situation is different now. At that time, there was no alternative. So, we have to look at it in a different way, because circumstances have changed.

8. Can you identify the nominal conjunction in the following sentence?
    I'll make sure I do it the instant I get home.

9. Which is the sentence connector below?
    It's a difficult problem. However, I prefer to solve it myself.

10. Can you identify the simple conjunctions in the sentence below?
    It was a nice meal, but I felt too full so I went and lay down on the settee.

11. Can you find the subordinating conjunction in the following sentence?
    I'll do it when I have a spare moment.

12. Which is the subordinator in the following sentence?
    After we had had a good swim in the large swimming pool at the bottom of the garden, we went home.

13. Can you identify the verbal conjunction in the sentence below?
    I've prepared a lovely salad, knowing you love salads so much.

What Goes with What? (answers on page 234)
Read the unpunctuated passage below very carefully, and then do the exercises which follow it.

Come in said Mr Smith smiling at me in the most welcoming manner What can we do for you today Well its something Ive been meaning to ask you for some time What is it then said Mr Smith Its about my leave Im due for leave in two weeks time and I wanted to ask you for a favour A favour We dont give favours in this company Mr Watson Favours are not our custom You know that as well as I do Yes I know I said but maybe you might consider an exception to the usual rule as one might say We make no exceptions Mr Watson Mr Smith said Not even for you

1. Put in all the full-stops.

2. Put in all the commas.

3. Put in all the apostrophes.

4. Put in any exclamation marks.

5. Put in the question marks.

6. Put in the quotation marks.

7. The sentence below could do with a semi-colon. Where would you put it?
    I didn't go to see Mr Smith Mr Smith didn't come to see me either.

8. Place commas, semi-colons and a colon in the sentence below:
    I took the following articles shoes socks and underwear soap and toothpaste bread biscuits and some chocolate.

9. Use both brackets and dashes in the sentence below:
    Tom, a friend of mine who isn't these days? of many years' standing, ran down the road shouting at the top of his voice, too.

10. In the sentence below, were all the students who left the room over eighteen?

    All the students, who were over eighteen, left the room.

11. In the following sentence, did all of the soldiers who came from Liverpool get killed?

    Thirty of the soldiers who came from Liverpool were killed.

12. Read the following sentence carefully:

    He said that I said it but he said that I said it because he said it and he didn't want anyone to know he said what he said I said.

    Now, rewrite the sentence and punctuate it by completing the following:

    Because he didn't ... ... that he ... ... it he said ... I ... ... it

Passages for Study

By now, you should be able to talk about the grammar of English with a reasonable degree of confidence. Nevertheless, how well and how quickly you learn to use grammatical terminology is entirely up to you. You may wish to go back and re-read some of the chapters, and rework some of the exercises. Try and build up your personal confidence, and try not to be impatient with yourself. Remember: you are not competing with anyone else. This is a self-study programme and you should set your own goals.

From now on, you will be given passages to study and comment on. You should read each passage through carefully first, to make sure you understand it. Try and decide what kind of English you are dealing with: formal or informal, fiction or non-fiction, and so on. Then, when you think you are ready, answer the questions which follow each passage.

Passage 1: Car Hire

We didn't damage the car. And it was returned with a tank full of petrol. The car-hire had been rather expensive, but worth it. But now, in a heavy Italian accent, a bored booking-clerk was telling us that our credit card would be debited for a further 110 euros. We were hot, tired, and now exasperated. 110 euros! Why? What for?

You may well ask. And so might the irate English lady who was being told she was having 700 euros deducted from her account. 'That's more than I pay for a year's car insurance at home,' she was angrily shouting.

I have in front of me the car-hire form, in Italian, which tells me that this money has been deducted for 'Addebiti Diversi'. Add a bit, indeed. And it certainly makes for a nice diversion.

Curious, I ring the car-hire firm in Norwich. Why did we have to pay this extra amount when we returned our car? No damage was done, the tank was full of petrol, and we paid for the hire-car as part of our holiday booking. 'I don't know, sir. I suggest you ring this number.'

So I do. A recorded female voice recites a list of touch-phone numbers to choose from, and I choose 'General Enquiries'. I tell General Enquiries about my problem and she puts me through to 'Invoices'. There is a delay while I am entertained to some light music. Finally, a clear Irish voice wishes me good morning and asks if she can help. Can I give her the reference number on the car-hire form? I assume she refers to the 'Fattura Ricevuta Fiscale' but don't try to pronounce it.

'Have you got a reference number there beginning with 343?' she asks. I scan a host of numbers and find it at last.

(answers on page 235)

1. Is the style of this passage formal or informal?

2. What contractions can you find in the first paragraph?

3. How many of the sentences in this paragraph begin with conjunctions?

4. Can you identify the modal auxiliaries in the second paragraph?

5. Can you find an example of the passive form of the past continuous in this paragraph?

6. There is a comparative, too. Which is it?

7. What part of speech is 'in front of' in paragraph three?

8. What two kinds of clauses are contained in the words 'which tells me that this money has been deducted'?

9. The prepositional phrase "for 'Addebiti Diversi'" could also be described as what?

10. An anaphoric device is used in the last sentence of the third paragraph. Which is it?

11. Can you identify the two compound nouns in the fifth paragraph?

12. How would you classify 'so' in 'So I do'?

13. What is the dominant tense in the last paragraph?

14. How many co-ordinate clauses can you find in the fifth paragraph?

Passage 2: Edith Cavell

On 12th October 1915, Edith Cavell was executed by the German military authorities in Brussels. She was shot at the Tir Nationale (the National Rifle Range). Her crime? Helping to save the lives of around 200 allied soldiers. Before her execution, she said: "I expected my sentence and I believe it was just." As far as she was concerned, she had abused her position as a nurse with the Red Cross which then, as it does now, carried out its relief work from a position of political neutrality.

After her execution, Edith was hurriedly buried nearby and a plain wooden cross was erected over her grave. Part of this cross can still be seen at Swardeston church. At the end of the war, her remains were carried to Westminster Abbey for a special memorial service. This took place on 25th May, 1919. But her remains were finally interred outside Norwich cathedral, at a spot called 'Life's Green' in the Cathedral Close. Her statue can be seen to this day, in Tombland, just outside the cathedral walls.

Edith Cavell has always exerted a fascination on those who have happened to come across her story. Anna Neagle starred in a film about her, and Joan Plowright appeared in a successful West End play about her, called 'Cavell'. She is, like that other martyr Dietrich Bonhoeffer, a twentieth century icon.

Maybe the clue to the mystery of this brave woman lies in her words, written not long before her death and after she had been sentenced: "I realise that patriotism is not enough. I must have no hatred or bitterness towards anyone." These are extraordinary words from someone about to face execution, and they came from someone whose Christianity had always been unselfconscious and practical. She had never been obviously 'pious'.

(answers on page 236)

1. What register is this passage in?

2. How many phrasal verbs can you find here, and which are they?

3. What examples of the passive can you find?

4. Put the short elliptical interrogative sentence in the first paragraph into its full form.

5. Is the sentence beginning with a participle form in the first paragraph a phrase or a clause?

6. How would you classify the clause beginning 'as far as' in the first paragraph?

7. Can you identify the example of the past perfect tense in the last sentence of the first paragraph?

8. How would you classify the phrase 'after her execution' in the first sentence of the second paragraph?

9. What part of speech is 'nearby'?

10. Can you identify the main clause in the sentence beginning 'at the end of the war'?

11. 'At a spot called "Life's Green" in the Cathedral Close' consists of two main groups. Can you say what they are?

12. In the phrase 'just outside', how would you describe the word 'just'?

13. The pronouns 'her' and 'she' in the third paragraph are examples of what kind of reference?

14. In the final paragraph, 'her words' are also an example of a certain kind of reference. What kind of reference?

15. What kind of auxiliary verb is 'must' in the last paragraph?

16. What kind of adjective is the word 'these'?

17. What part of the last sentence is the phrase 'obviously pious'?

Passage 3: Getting Lost

It was raining steadily. Janet tried to make out the names of the streets through the blurred windscreen, but it was very difficult. Tom, meanwhile, drove on and on, waiting for Janet to decide which street she wanted him to turn into.

"She said it was 'Slipper Street'," Janet said. "There doesn't seem to be a 'Slipper' Street."

"I thought you said it was 'Silver' Street," Tom said, quietly.

"It was 'Slipper' Street," Janet said, defiantly. "I know it was."

"Why don't you look on the map?" Tom said.

"Can you see it?" shouted Janet, thrusting the map under his face.

"I'm driving," Tom said. "I can't look at the map and drive at the same time."

"I thought you could do anything. Anything you wanted to. Nothing was too difficult for the great Tom Griffin."

"Most things," Tom said. "Not everything. One must draw the line somewhere."

"Oh, damn, damn, damn!"

"Steady, old girl," Tom said, chuckling.

"Don't you dare call me 'old girl'," Janet said. "I'm not one of your vintage cars."

They drove on in silence.

"There it is," Tom said. "Silver Street."

"It's not the right name," Janet protested.

(answers on page 237)

1. Is this passage fiction or non-fiction?

2. What tense does the passage begin with?

3. Write down the three infinitives which occur in the first paragraph.

4. How are quotation marks used to show stress when the street is named?

5. Where is an exclamation mark used to good effect?

6. How many contractions can you find, and what are they?

7. How would you classify the word 'very' in the first paragraph?

8. Can you describe the separate items in the sentence "There doesn't seem to be a 'Slipper' Street"?

9. How would you describe the word 'too' in 'too difficult'?

10. How would you classify the words 'anything' and 'nothing'?

11. Describe the items in: "Steady, old girl," Tom said, chuckling".

12. Do the same with 'They drove on in silence'.

13. Explain the verbal parts of "Don't you dare call me 'old girl' ".

14. What is 'most' in the phrase 'most things'?

15. In the sentence "I can't look at the map", how would you describe 'can't'?

16. What do you think the difference is between 'it's not' and 'it isn't'?

17. What is the difference between 'look at the map' and 'look on the map'?

18. How would you describe the clauses in 'I thought you said it was'?

19. Classify the two main parts of 'thrusting the map under his face'.

20. What is 'somewhere'?

Passage 4: You're Not Getting Any Younger

"You've got to be sensible about this, mother," Gerry said.

"I've always been sensible, Gerry. You know that," Mrs Thompson said.

"But you can't look after yourself properly. You know that very well."

"Who cooked your lunch?" said Mrs Thompson. "Who made up your bed? Who put the central heating on to make sure your room warmed up?"

"Yes, I know that mother, but there are other things?"

"What things?"

"Well, you're not getting any younger, mother."

"Neither are you, dear. How old are you now? Fifty-six? And you know you shouldn't smoke like you do. Not with your heart trouble."

"Stop changing the subject, mother. If you have a fall, or a stroke or something, who's going to look after you? I think you'd be much better off in a Home."

"We'll worry about that when the time comes," said Mrs Thompson. "If it does. And who's going to look after you, if you have a heart attack? Me, of course."

"What do you mean?"

"Well, since Marilyn left you, you've had to fend for yourself. And you don't seem to find it easy, dear, if you don't mind my saying so. I sometimes wonder whether it wouldn't be best if you came here to live with me. You can come home whenever you like. You know that."

"I'm talking about you mother."

"I'm just a little deaf, dear. It's nothing serious," she said, smiling.

(answers on page 238)

1. List the contractions in this passage.

2. Find four different examples of interrogative pronouns introducing questions.

3. Now list two different examples of demonstrative pronouns.

210

4. What difference does the comma after 'this' make in the first line?

5. How would you classify the two-word verb 'put on' in 'put the central heating on'?

6. Explain the anaphoric reference of the pronoun 'that' in line 2.

7. Substitute a more formal conjunction for 'but' in line 4.

8. Why is 'make up' in 'make up your bed' a phrasal verb and not a prepositional two-word verb?

9. Substitute a more formal verb for the verb 'get' in 'getting younger'.

10. Why is 'neither' in 'neither are you, dear' called a 'co-ordinating conjunction'?

11. Rewrite the three parts of 'If you have a fall, or a stroke, or something' so that you have three fully formed adverbial clauses of condition.

12. Now rewrite 'if you have a fall' as a subjunctive clause using 'were' and an infinitive.

13. Does "we'll" stand for 'we will' or 'we shall'?

14. Give an alternative future form for the phrase 'who's going to look after you?'

15. Is the relative pronoun 'what' used interrogatively in 'What do you mean?' anaphoric, cataphoric, or both?

16. In the sentence 'Well, since Marilyn left you, you've had to fend for yourself', which is the main clause?

17. Is the clause 'whether it wouldn't be best' an adverbial clause or a noun clause? Why?

Passage 5: The House

The house was situated on the corner of a quiet street, within walking distance of the city centre. The high wooden fence in front of the house, which surmounted a white wall, made it very private, and the black wrought iron gates gave it an air of distinction. Through the gates, you could see a paved courtyard and, beyond the courtyard, the house itself.

The house was painted white, with a mahogany-coloured door and windows. There was an integral garage at the side which had mahogany-coloured double doors. The colours blended nicely and created a subdued tasteful effect, which was enhanced by the raised beds of evergreen shrubs near the fence, and the bed of heathers surrounded by cobbles in front of the main window.

It was a semi-detached house, with all its separate rooms intact and carefully decorated in mild, pastel colours. The kitchen was quite large, and looked out onto a walled garden with yet more evergreen shrubs, and an ancient apple tree. There was a pretty lawn in the centre, and flagstone paths. A shed was half-hidden behind the apple tree.

Immediately outside the rear windows, beyond the kitchen, there was a partly covered veranda. The open part of the veranda was flagged and bounded by a low curtain wall. Two low brick pillars framed the steps that led down onto the lawn.

(answers on page 239)

1. What is the infinitive of 'was situated'?

2. What kind of phrase is 'within walking distance'?

3. What kind of phrase is 'of the city centre'?

4. Which group of words is the subject of the second sentence in the first paragraph?

5. The second sentence in the first paragraph contains the word 'and'. How would you describe this word and its function?

6. How would you describe the phrases 'high wooden fence' and 'black wrought iron gates'?

7. Insert commas in the two phrases above. Is any other punctuation needed?

8. In the first sentence of the second paragraph, how would you classify 'with a mahogany-coloured door and windows'?

9. 'Subdue' is a transitive verb, so what is 'subdued' in the third sentence of the second paragraph?

10. In the same sentence, what part of speech is the word 'by' and does it belong with 'enhanced' or 'the raised beds'?

11. In the third paragraph, is 'its' correctly punctuated? Explain.

12. How would you classify 'quite' in 'quite large'

13. Explain the verbal phrase 'looked out onto'.

14. How would you classify the word 'yet' in the second sentence of the third paragraph?

15. Identify and explain the articles in the third paragraph.

16. Explain the phrase 'immediately outside'.

17. Should 'partly covered' and 'open part' be hyphenated? Why?

18. How would you describe 'flagged and bounded'?

19. Does 'two low brick pillars' need punctuating?

20. How many clauses are there in the last sentence? What are they?

Passage 6: Alternative Medicine

It is very common to meet people who have lost faith in their family doctor and conventional medicine and have relied on osteopaths, for example, or practitioners in Chinese medicine to solve their health problems. But how safe are these remedies and how professional are those who provide alternative therapies?

According to an independent health care organisation which has adopted the name Dr Foster and is based at Exeter University, all practitioners in complementary or alternative medicine should satisfy five basic conditions before they can be considered truly professional and safe. According to Dr Foster, patients need to know how many sessions of treatment are necessary for their condition; what the treatment will involve; how much the treatment will cost and how it should be paid for; what side-effects there might be; and how to contact the practitioner outside clinic hours.

A recently published Times Complementary Therapists Guide listed complementary therapists who were members of highly regulated professional organisations and also listed the Dr Foster conditions that they satisfied. Two of those listed are members of The Clinic in High Road, Norwich. They are John Smith, an osteopath, and Peter Jones, an acupuncturist. But neither of them fulfil all five conditions, and no other therapists at the clinic are in the Guide.

(answers on page 241)

1. What kind of reference is the pronoun 'it' in the first sentence?

2. What verb tense is 'have lost'?

3. Which group of words forms the object of this verb?

4. How would you classify the phrase 'for example'?

5. Identify the second infinitive in this sentence and its object.

6. Explain the group 'but how safe' in the second sentence.

7. Which is the main clause in the first sentence of the second paragraph?

8. How would you describe 'according to an independent health care organisation'?

9. Define the verb form 'should' in this sentence.

10. What form of the verb is 'can be considered'?

11. Explain the form 'need to know' in the next sentence.

12. What kind of phrase is 'for their condition'?

13. Explain the use of semi-colons in this sentence.

14. Which group of words forms the subject of the first sentence in the last paragraph?

15. Which group of words forms the object of the verb 'listed'?

16. Explain the structure of the rest of this sentence, beginning with the word 'and'.

17. Explain the capitalisation in the second sentence of the last paragraph.

18. Which is the connective in the next sentence, and what kind of connective is it?

19. Expand 'an osteopath' to create a relative clause beginning with the correct relative pronoun.

20. Explain the grammar of 'and no other therapists at the clinic are in the Guide'.

21. Why does the word 'guide' begin with a capital letter?

Passage 7: Huntingdonshire

Well, where is it? You know where Rutland is, because it's back on the map. But Hunts? That's a different matter.

Of course, Huntingdonshire has always produced its famous names. Every school child is made familiar with the name of Oliver Cromwell, who was a native of the county town, even if he or she soon forgets what he was famous for. And in modern times, John Major, who succeeded Margaret Thatcher as prime minister, was the local MP. And there were others, like Samuel Pepys, William Cowper, and George Herbert, whose names have always been associated with what was the second smallest county in England.

I say 'was' because, as anyone who consults a modern atlas of Great Britain will soon discover, Huntingdonshire no longer exists. Except as an administrative area within Cambridgeshire, that is. So where was it?

The county town of Huntingdon has now taken second place to its more famous cousin, Cambridge, and anyone travelling by car or cycle from Cambridge towards St Neots will, of necessity, cross what was originally the county boundary between Cambridgeshire and Huntingdonshire. Although the village is now by-passed, Eltisley, with its lovely village green, still used for local cricket matches, used to be on the main Cambridge to St Neots road and was very close to the county boundary. But the next village, Croxton, was the closest Cambridgeshire village to Huntingdonshire. The pub, 'The Spread Eagle', is no longer there but, once upon a time, it reminded travellers that they were about to enter 'foreign' country.

Find the earliest forms of the following in the passage above (answers on page 242):

1. A superlative adjective.

2. A comparative adjective.

3. An intensifier.

4. A participial adjective.

5. An adverb clause of condition.

6. An adverb clause of reason.

7. An adverb clause of place.

8. An adverb of place.

9. An adverb of frequency.

10. An adverb of time.

11. An adjectival clause.

12. A noun clause.

13. A co-ordinate clause.

14. A relative clause.

15. The simple past tense.

16. The present perfect tense.

17. The simple present tense.

18. The present passive.

19. A demonstrative pronoun.

20. A possessive pronoun.

21. A noun clause as object.

22. A proper noun.

23. A compound noun.

A Final Test (answers on page 243)

Here is a final test for you which should give you a clear idea of what you have now learned and what you are still not sure about. The test includes most of the grammatical terms used in this book.

A. Identify the tenses in the following examples:

1. *She is listening.*

2. *John has finished.*

3. *Alan speaks four languages.*

4. *We had been travelling for three days.*

5. *In two weeks' time, I shall have been living here for nine years.*

6. *What will you do?*

7. *Maureen had graduated two years earlier.*

8. *I shall be waiting for you.*

9. *The part will have finished by now.*

10. *He left on Tuesday.*

11. *They were laughing at us.*

12. *I've been to the supermarket.*

B. Identify the types of clause in the following examples:

1. *They wanted to know what the answer was.*

2. *The man who taught me English has died.*

3. *I lived in the city suburbs, where there aren't many buses.*

C. What type of adverb clauses can you identify in the following examples?

1. *It was situated in the south of the country, where the big factories are.*

2. *Come after dinner, when everything is much quieter.*

3. *I couldn't come, because I didn't feel well.*

4. *He came to see us as often as he could.*

5. *I'll do it if you lend me a hand.*

6. *They acted as if they intended to win.*

D. How would you classify the following verb parts?

1. *might*

2. *to run*

3. *laughing*

4. *lived*

E. Which of these verbs are transitive, which are intransitive and which are both?

1. *shoot*

2. *give*

3. *study*

4. *pause*

5.   *grin*

F.   Identify the main verb in these sentences:

1.   *He ought to be more careful.*

2.   *In the sudden darkness, there was not a sound to be heard.*

3.   *He really ought not to have done it.*

G.   In the following examples, which are the phrasal verbs?

1.   *Take off your shoes.*

2.   *The plane took off.*

3.   *Can you put me up tonight?*

4.   *Put it up the chimney.*

5.   *He wound me up.*

6.   *He wound the clock up.*

H.   Which of these verbs are active and which are passive?

1.   *She listened carefully.*

2.   *I have listened to everything.*

3.   *Everything has been written down.*

4.   *I have been listening.*

5.   *Has it been done yet?*

I. From the following list of adjectives, identify the comparatives, the superlatives, the participials, and the possessives:

shining; her; the biggest; ragged; warmer; their; nicer; waning

J. From this list of adverbials, identify the adverbials of degree, duration, frequency, manner, place, and time:

now; easily; partly; often; here; for two hours

K. Read the following sentence:

He did the job well, but hadn't finished it by the time I came home.

Identify the following:

1. The adverb.

2. The verbs in the simple past tense.

3. The two personal pronouns.

4. The conjunction.

5. The impersonal pronoun.

6. The verb in the past perfect tense.

7. The prepositional phrase.

8. The main clause.

9. The subordinate clauses and their type.

10. The object of the verb *came*.

L.   Identify the types of noun in this list:

thought; house; London; head-piece

M.   Which of these nouns are countable?

milk; car; desk; water; sheep

N.   What type are the following phrases?

1.   *by the river*

2.   *very difficult*

3.   *as quickly as possible*

4.   *the man in the pub*

O.   Complete this passage by filling in the blanks:

Spoken language can be described by using a special alphabet called the ... alphabet. This alphabet uses symbols to represent the ... sounds and the ... sounds in the language, as well as the combined vowels, or ... The rise and fall, or ... , can also be represented. Basically, each language has a finite number of sounds used to distinguish words, and these sounds are called ... .

P.   Put these terms in their correct order, from the smallest element to the largest:

phrase; morpheme; sentence; lexical item; clause; paragraph

Q.   Identify the types of pronoun below:

1.   *this*

2.   *their*

3. *them*

4. *it*

5. *who*

6. *what?*

R. Which of these phrases are examples of postmodification and which of premodification?

1. *the man with the red hat*

2. *the angry looking lady*

3. *the trouble we'd taken*

4. *one for the road*

S. Which of the above are attributive and which are predicative?

T. Study this list of words:

on Tuesday; basically; are listening; to; bus; she is beautiful; all the houses

Now identify:

1. An adverb of degree.

2. A countable noun.

3. An example of concord.

4. An adjunct.

5. An example of the copula.

6. An example of an open class word.

7. An example of a closed class word.

8. An example of aspect.

9. A verb phrase.

10. A prepositional phrase.

U. Study this list of words and phrases:

   bill; uncover; out of order; he's a teacher; therefore; alone; with; immediately; in order that

Now identify:

1. A prefix.

2. A homonym.

3. A prepositional complement.

4. A sentence connector.

5. An adverbial conjunction.

6. A predicative only adjective.

7. A subordinator.

8. A structural word.

9. A subject complement.

10. A conjunct.

18

Answers to Exercises

Basics

1. Verbs: *find; run; running; slide; carry*
    Adverbs: *easily; quickly; fast; slowly; calmly*

2. *af*ter; im**possible**; co**rrect**; **marry**; under**line**; **fore**cast; cour**age**ously; **din**ner; **mu**sical; **sim**ilar

3. *in the end; for the time being; the big house; here is the car; over the moon; high and dry; the one at the end; when the time came; not there; take it or leave it*

4. *afternoon* (4); *watch* (1); *settee* (3); *piece* (3); *house* (3); *football* (3); *guard* (2); *news* (1); *marmalade* (4); *cheese* (3)

5. *afternoon* (5); *watch* (4); *settee* (3); *piece* (2); *house* (2); *football* (5); *guard* (3); *news* (3); *marmalade* (5); *cheese* (3)

6. *afternoon* (3); *watch* (1); *settee* (2); *piece* (1); *house* (1); *football* (2); *guard* (1); *news* (1); *marmalade* (3); *cheese* (1)

7. *sea/see; there/their; here/hear; hair/hare; saw/sore; rain/rein*

8. Four: *came; were coming; comes; had come*

225

9. *He stood and waited. Then he saw them.*

10. *the clock says five; all men are equal; nine apples; time flies; he is washing himself; those are their bags; this is it; the soldiers are coming; take these presents home; Mary and Jane are sisters*

11. *horses*; cows; sing**ing**; th**eir**; m**ine**; races; parties; lazy; footballers; c**aught**

Nuts and Bolts
1. *woman; children; toast; car; policeman; teacher*

2. *silence; friendship; fear; hunger; night; darkness*

3. *mother; tea; student; window; angel*

4. *large; comfortable; warm; dizzy; muddy*

5. *lovely* (adjective); *yellow* (adjective); *quickly* (adverb); *misery* (noun); *usefully* (adverb); *utility* (noun); *strange* (adjective); *tidily* (adverb); *horse* (noun); *nature* (noun)

6. *yesterday; went; married; saw; studied*

7. *this morning; every day; buys; cycling; at present; jumps; hello; sleeps*

8.   (d) Watch this space.
     (f) I saw him in the shop yesterday morning.
     (h) Yes, I do.
     (i) Come into the garden with me and see.

Sorting Things Out
1. *table* (neuter); *girl* (feminine); *waitress* (feminine); *hero* (masculine); *emperor* (masculine); *queen* (feminine); *vixen* (feminine); *dinner* (neuter); *tree* (neuter)

2. *is, return; grammar, readers, subject, return; interesting, enjoyable*

3. *trees; economics; the nation's; China*

4. *prayers; a car; crowds; roses; litres*

5. *the ball; the houses; the cup*

6. *Mary; her; she; policeman*

7. *bought* (three); *bike* (three); *laughing* (five); *motor* (four); *hill* (three); *light* (three); *mine* (three)

8. *planes; they; soldiers; arches*

9. *their; father's; her; William's*

10. **in**direct; **un**do; **up**turn; **out**going; **on**set; **post**script

11. *he; their; I; his; ourselves; it*

12. *protect from harm*

13. *peach; laughter; status; series; crowd; pie*

14. *larfter; theyer; iznit*

15. *cats; cheese; you; I*

Parts of the Sentence
1. *hard*

2. *with great courage and tenacity*

3. **Three**

4. **Two**

5. *as if she was about to be sick*

6. *Then he switched it on and saw a man who was running away from the car.*

7. *Some liked the idea but some hated it.*

8. Four: *and; but; so; and*

9. *she asked us inside/(she) told us to sit down*

10. *ai; ie; i; eo; iou; oy; oi* (in their pronounced forms)

11. *line/line; tear/tear*

12. *Jack walked slowly towards the burglar*

13. *car; door; boot*

14. Two: *learn* and the ending *ing*

15. *at one o'clock exactly; having promised his father very seriously*

16. Four: *daylight; friendship; seldom; courtesy*

17. *my mother*

18. *at night; with my best friend*

19. *on; by; in; at*

Building the Sentence

1. *which loves creamy milk*

2. yesterday (time); *often* (frequency); *there* (place); *while* (duration); *there* (place)

3. *cows; grass; cow; hay; farm; house; years*

4. *dog; bird; cow*

5. Definite: *the; the; the; the*
   Indefinite: *a; some*

6. *this; that; those; these; that; that*

7. *all; some*

8. Finite: *Imagine going home; I needed to continue my journey*
   Non-finite: *to sit by the fire; to sleep in the warm*

9. *to sit; to sleep; to continue*

10. Noun clause: *the money he had earned*
    Noun phrase: *a rich but disappointed man*

Expanding the Parts

1. *with wonderful sensitivity*

2. *when the lesson had finished*

3. *slowly; suddenly; when the smoke had cleared*

4. *exhausted; was; was; slept; awoke*
   [Note: The verb 'to walk' can be intransitive but it is transitive here.]

5. *with dark hair; little*

6. *painted white*

7. *my little Polish*

8. *when the rain had stopped; which was in a sorry state*

9. *hammered*

10. *fingers* (noun); *beautiful* (adjective); *slowly* (adverb); *on* (preposition); *swim* (verb)

The Importance of the Verb

1. *should; haven't*

2. *haven't*

3. *looks*

4. adjective; adjective; noun

5. future

6. *shall be; will be; shouldn't*

7. *fought; found; felt*

8. *passed; revise*

9. *running; passed*

10. *passed*

11. Three: past continuous; past perfect; past simple

12. *she's coming*

13. *leaving; making*

14. *like; like; like*

15. Four: *is going dark; is still shining; can't say; is*

16. *was; drove; left; sold; went*

17. Two: *can't; I've*

More About the Verb

1. The second: *they weren't sure*

2. *I'm trying*: present continuous
   I've always tried: present perfect
   I try: present simple
   I've been trying: present perfect continuous
   I shall always try: future simple
   I shall be trying: future continuous
   I expect: present simple
   I'll have been trying: future perfect continuous
   I tried: past simple
   I always did: past simple
   You know: present simple
   I'll have tried: future perfect
   I was trying: past continuous
   we got: past simple
   I'd tried: past perfect
   I'd always been trying: past perfect continuous
   you know: present simple

3. Aspect

4. Conjugation

5. Second person singular

6. First person plural

7. Imperative

8. *is*

9. Mood

10. *put up with; up with*

11. *Whatever his parents said, it certainly shouldn't have been put up with*

12. Active: *tested*
    Passive: *had to be tested*

13. Perfective

14. Present participle

15. *were*

16. *get by*

17. *usage*

Adjectives and Description
1. *little brown*

2. *taller; higher*

3. *income tax return*

4. *very; extremely*

5. Three comparatives: *nicer; more brightly; better*
   Three nominals: *morning; yesterday; sun*

6. *broken*

7. *gathering*

8. *red and crisp*

9. *best; cheapest; hottest*

How Adverbs Can Help
1. *if you promise to return it*

2. *whenever you can find the time*

3. *as if she owned the place*

4. *where the old cinema used to be*

5. *because it's so peaceful*

6. *so I missed the early train*

7. *when the bells rang*

8. *carefully*

9. *We play tennis every Tuesday.*

10. *Very slowly and deliberately, the gunman fired two shots.*

11. *She is, of course, the college principal.*

12. *and; at; into*

Tying Things Together: Prepositions

1. *to; the; and; me; a; of*

2. *out of*

3. *lived; detached; house; large; back; garden*

4. *put up with*

5. *took off*

6. *at the front; to the back*

7. *send for*

8. *into (the room); on (a chair); on (the table); near (the table); on (the floor); to (the window); on (the gravel); at (me)*

Joining Things Up: Conjunctions

1. *nevertheless*

2. *However; Therefore*

3. *so that*

4. *As a result*

5. Four: *she kept; the box; firmly; closed*

6. *and*

7. *What I said; At that time; So*

8. *the instant*

9. *However*

10. *but; so; and*

11. *when*

12. *after*

13. *knowing*

What Goes with What?
1-6:

"Come in," said Mr Smith, *smiling at me in the most welcoming manner. "What can we do for you today?"*

"Well, it's something I've been meaning to ask you for some time."

"What is it then?" said Mr Smith.

"It's about my leave. I'm due for leave in two weeks' time and I wanted to ask you for a favour."

"A favour! We don't give favours in this company, Mr Watson. Favours are not our custom. You know that as well as I do."

"Yes, I know," I said, "but maybe you might consider an exception to the usual rule, as one might say."

"We make no exceptions, Mr Watson," Mr Smith said. "Not even for you."

7. *I didn't go to see Mr Smith; Mr Smith didn't come to see me either.*

8. *I took the following articles: shoes, socks, and underwear; soap and toothpaste; bread, biscuits, and some chocolate.*
   [Note: Some people prefer to omit the commas before *and*.]

9. *Tom, a friend of mine (who isn't these days?) of many years' standing, ran down the road shouting – at the top of his voice, too.*

10. Yes, they were.

11. No.

12. *Because he didn't want anyone to know that he had said it, he said that I had said it.*

Passage 1
1. Informal.

2. *didn't*

3. Two.

4. *may; might*

5. *was being told*

6. *more*

7. A prepositional phrase.

235

8. Adjective and noun.

9. An adjunct.

10. *it*

11. *touch-phone; General Enquiries*

12. A sentence connector.

13. Present simple.

14. Two in the second sentence. Two in the third sentence. Two in the fifth sentence. Two in the last sentence.

Passage 2
1. Formal.

2. *carry out*

3. *was executed; was shot; was concerned; was buried; was erected; can be seen; were carried; were interred; can be seen; had been sentenced*

4. *What was her crime?*

5. A phrase.

6. Adverbial clause of degree.

7. *she had abused*

8. Adverbial phrase of time.

9. Adverb.

10. *her remains were carried to Westminster Abbey*

11. Adverbial phrase of place: *At a spot*
    Participial adjective phrase: *called 'Life's Green'*

12. Intensifier, modifying the adverb *outside*.

13. Anaphoric.

14. Cataphoric.

15. Modal.

16. Demonstrative.

17. Complement.

Passage 3

1. Fiction.

2. Past continuous.

3. *to make out; to decide; to turn into*

4. By using single quotation marks for the word.

5. *Oh, damn, damn, damn!*

6. Seven: *doesn't; don't; I'm; can't; don't; I'm; it's*

7. Intensifier.

8. Introductory *there* followed by negative auxiliary *do* in the present simple tense, followed by the intransitive verb *seem*, followed by the infinitive *to be*, followed by the indefinite article *a* modifying the compound proper noun *Silver Street*.

9. Intensifier.

10. Impersonal pronouns.

11. Imperative *steady* followed by adjective *old* premodifying noun *girl* followed by proper noun *Tom* followed by past simple form of verb *say* followed by present participle of verb *chuckle*.

12. Third person plural pronoun *they* followed by past simple of verb *drive* followed by adverbial *on* modifying the previous verb, followed by adverbial phrase of manner *in silence*.

13. Negative imperative of the auxiliary verb *do* used with the main verb *dare* modifying the bare infinitive of the verb *call*.

14. Superlative adjective.

15. Modal auxiliary.

16. The full form of the negative is more emphatic.

17. *look at* is a two-word verb, whereas *look on* is a verb followed by a prepositional adverb.

18. A main clause *I thought* followed by a noun clause as object *you said* which is followed by a further noun clause *it was*.

19. Participial phrase *thrusting the map* followed by adverbial phrase *under his face*.

20. An adverb of place.

Passage 4
1. *you've; I've; can't; you're; shouldn't; who's; you'd; we'll; who's; you've; don't; don't; wouldn't; I'm; I'm; it's*

2. *who?; what?; how?; who's?*

238

3. *this; that*

4. It separates the statement and the person addressed.

5. A phrasal verb.

6. It refers back to *I've always been sensible.*

7. *however*

8. Because the object can come between the verb and the particle.

9. *becoming*

10. Because it connects with, and repeats, *you are not getting any younger.*

11. *If you have a fall, or if you have a stroke, or if you have something similar*

12. *Were you to have a fall*

13. *we shall*

14. *who will look after you?*

15. Both: it refers to what Mrs Thompson said and to any future explanation.

16. *you've had to fend for yourself*

17. It's a noun clause: object of the verb *wonder (wonder what?).*

Passage 5
1. *to be situated*

2. Adverbial.

3. Prepositional.

4. *The high wooden fence in front of the house, which surmounted a white wall*

5. A coordinating conjunction.

6. Noun phrases.

7. *high, wooden fence; black, wrought-iron gates (hyphen between wrought and iron)*

8. An adjectival phrase post-modifying the noun house.

9. A participial adjective.

10. An adverbial belonging with *enhanced.*

11. Yes. There is no apostrophe in *its* when used possessively.

12. It is an intensifier.

13. Verb followed by an adverb followed by a preposition.

14. An intensifier.

15. 'a semi-detached house' (a type: general); '*the* kitchen' (this particular one); '*a* walled garden' (a type: general); '*an* ancient apple tree' (type: general); '*a* pretty lawn' (type: general); '*the* centre' (this particular place); '*a* shed (type of building); '*the* apple tree' (this particular one)

16. Adverbial premodifier of the adverb *outside.*

17. *partly covered* should be hyphenated, since the two words form a compound adjective, but *open part* consists of a noun which is premodified by the adjective *open*.

18. They are participial adjectives.

19. Yes. It should be *two, low, brick pillars*, since the adjectives *two* and *low* describe both the number and the type of 'brick pillar'.

20. Two: *Two low brick pillars framed the steps* (main clause) *that led down onto the lawn* (subordinate adjective clause, introduced by a relative pronoun and describing the noun *steps*.

Passage 6

1. Cataphoric.

2. Present perfect.

3. *faith in their family doctor and conventional medicine*

4. A connecting adverbial phrase.

5. *to solve their health problems*

6. Conjunction followed by an interrogative adverb modifying the adjective *safe*.

7. *All practitioners in complementary medicine or alternative medicine should satisfy five basic conditions.*

8. A participial phrase.

9. Modal auxiliary.

10. Passive, introduced by a modal auxiliary.

11. Present simple form of the verb *need* followed by the infinitive of the verb *know*.

12. Prepositional.

13. The semi-colons are used to separate the five separate things which patients need to know.

14. *A recently published Times Complementary Therapists Guide*

15. *complementary therapists who were members of highly regulated professional organisations*

16. The conjunction *and* introduces a co-ordinate clause with *listed* as its main verb.

17. The capitals are used for proper nouns.

18. The connective is *and* and it is a simple conjunction.

19. *who is an osteopath*

20. This is a co-ordinate clause introduced by *and*.

21. Because it refers to a particular book.

Passage 7
1. *smallest*

2. *more famous*

3. *very*

4. *by-passed*

5. *if he or she forgets*

6. *because it's back on the map*

242

7. *where Rutland is*

8. *back*

9. *always*

10. *soon*

11. *who was a native of the county town*

12. *what he was famous for*

13. *anyone travelling by car or cycle from Cambridge towards St Neots will cross*

14. Same as 11.

15. *was*

16. *has always produced*

17. *is*

18. *is made*

19. *that*

20. *its*

21. *what he was famous for*

22. *Rutland*

23. *school child*

A Final Test
A.

1. The present continuous (or progressive).

2. The present perfect.

3. The present simple (or simple present).

4. The past perfect continuous (or progressive).

5. The future perfect continuous (or progressive).

6. The future simple (or simple future).

7. The past perfect.

8. The future continuous (or progressive).

9. The future perfect.

10. The past simple (or simple past).

11. The past continuous (or progressive).

12. The present perfect.

B.

1. Main clause. Subordinate noun clause.

2. Main clause. Embedded subordinate relative (or adjective) clause.

3. Main clause. Subordinate adverbial clause of place.

C.

1. Adverb clause of place.

2. Adverb clause of time.

3. Adverb clause of reason.

4. Adverb clause of frequency.

5. Adverb clause of condition.

6. Adverb clause of manner.

D.

1. Modal auxiliary.

2. Infinitive (with preposition).

3. Present participle.

4. Past participle.

E.

1. Both.

2. Transitive.

3. Both.

4. Intransitive.

5. Intransitive.

F.

1. *be*

2. *was*

3. *done*

G.

took off in 2; *put ... up* in 3; *wound ... up* in 5.

H.

1. Active.

2. Active.

3. Passive.

4. Active.

5. Passive.

I.

Comparatives: *warmer, nicer*

Superlatives: *the biggest*

Participials: *shining, ragged, waning*

Possessives: *her, their*

J.

Degree: *partly*

Duration: *for two hours*

Frequency: *often*

Manner: *easily*

Place: *here*

Time: *now*

K.

1. *well*

2. *did; came*

3. *he; I*

4. *but*

5. *it*

6. *hadn't finished*

7. *by the time*

8. *he did the job well*

9. *but hadn't finished it* (co-ordinate main clause); *by the time I came home* (subordinate adverbial clause of time)

10. *home*

L.

thought (abstract); *house* (common/concrete); *London* (proper); *head-piece* (compound)

M.

car and *desk*

N.

1. Prepositional.

2. Adjectival.

3. Adverbial.

4. Nominal.

O.

phonetic; vowel; consonant; diphthongs; intonation; phonemes

P.

morpheme; lexical item; phrase; clause; sentence; paragraph

Q.

1. Demonstrative.

2. Personal.

3. Personal.

4. Impersonal.

5. Relative.

6. Interrogative.

R.

1. Postmodification.

2. Premodification.

3. Postmodification.

4. Postmodification.

S.

2 is attributive; the rest are predicative.

T.

1. *basically*

2. *bus; houses*

3. *all the houses*

4. *on Tuesday*

5. *are listening*

6. *listening; bus; beautiful; houses*

7. *on; to; the*

8. *are listening; is beautiful*

9. *she is beautiful*

10. *on Tuesday*

U.

1. *un-*

2. *bill*

3. *out of order*

4. *therefore*

5. *immediately*

6. *alone*

7. *in order that*

8. *with*

9. *a teacher*

10. *therefore*

Index